Curiosity may have killed the cat, but it's perfectly safe for you to read these *Jeeves* titles...

Just Curious About History, Jeeves

And the upcoming

Just Curious About Science, Jeeves

Available from Pocket Books

T0109912

Did you know . . .

*a chipmunk can hold up to thirty-four nuts in
its cheeks?*

*an alligator's brain is about the size of a
human thumb?*

*chimps have been documented making war
against rival groups?*

some flowers smell like rotting meat?

*the blue whale has a heart the size of a
Volkswagen Beetle?*

**Well, now you do!
Look inside for even *more* answers. . . .**

JUST Curious ABOUT ANIMALS AND NATURE, Jeeves

Erin Barrett & Jack Mingo

With Illustrations by Marcos Sorensen and Spence Snyder

POCKET BOOKS
New York   London   Toronto   Sydney   Singapore

An *Original* Publication of POCKET BOOKS

 POCKET BOOKS, a division of Simon & Schuster, Inc.
1230 Avenue of the Americas, New York, NY 10020

ISBN-13: 978-0-7434-2710-4

First Pocket Books trade paperback printing August 2002

10 9 8 7 6 5 4 3 2 1

POCKET and colophon are registered trademarks of
Simon & Schuster, Inc.

For information regarding special discounts for bulk purchases,
please contact Simon & Schuster Special Sales at 1-800-456-6798
or business@simonandschuster.com

Printed in the U.S.A.

ACKNOWLEDGMENTS

Special thanks to:

Amanda Ayers Barnett
Paolo Pepe
Donna O'Neill
Kathlyn McGreevy
Marcos Sorensen
Spencer Snyder
Penny Finnie
Jacquie Harrison
Steve Berkowitz
John Dollison
Anne Kinney
Jerry & Lynn Barrett
Elana Mingo
Eric Childs
Georgia Hamner
Jackson Hamner

Contents

From THE
Authors

Here we are again, thrilled to be asked to put together another book for Ask Jeeves. This is the third in the series, after *Just Curious, Jeeves* and *Just Curious About History, Jeeves,* both available at bookstores everywhere.

As with the other two books, we went to our river of inspiration, the secret backstage "peek box," where we watched questions rush in from all over the world like a waterfall of curiosity. As you probably know, Ask Jeeves (www.ask.com) is one of the most popular websites on the Internet, receiving an average of 5 million questions every single day of the year. True, most of them are pretty straightforward ("Where can I buy an ant farm?" "Where can I find the lyrics to World War I songs?" "What is the weather in Antarctica like?"), and the computerized butler handles them with his usual finesse.

However, we occasionally see a rare one that hits us where it counts, in the heart and mind. Clearly it has come from a kindred soul, a curious spirit. Sometimes the questions come from people just thinking about stuff in the middle of the night. Sometimes they're the result of the final mind-numbing round of a favorite trivia game, or a group of friends arguing facts at a party, or a kid trying to refute a bossy older sibling. These are the questions we try to pick out and answer in these books.

Thanks to all who have gone to Ask Jeeves to pose your intriguing, unexpected, and sometimes just plain weird questions. Because of you, we now know how big an alligator's brain is (about the size of your thumb); how many mosquito bites it would take to completely drain your blood (if you're of average height, 1.12 million); whether lemmings are suicidal (they aren't)–and so many more fascinating facts that our larger-than-thumb-size brains hurt just thinking about it.

One thing we found interesting while working on *Just Curious About Animals and Nature, Jeeves* is how much other species resemble human beings in some very important ways. But what's even more interesting is how completely unlike us they are in other ways. It's humbling. Sure, we could teach other life-forms a thing or two (e.g., fetching, rolling over, shaking hands, conjugating verbs, splitting the atom). On the other hand, humans should also acknowledge how much we could learn from them as well. Who wouldn't want the patience of a redwood tree or the winter-proofing of the woolly bear caterpillar? Who wouldn't want to be able to fly like a seagull, swim like a dolphin, see like a hawk, swing through the trees like a gibbon, navigate like a salmon, or smell like a lion? (Better than smelling like a skunk, that's for sure.)

What about our role in society? Would we be better off with the single-mindedness of bees, the individualism of tigers, or the aggressiveness of chimps? Would matriarchs be any less oppressive than patriarchs?

While researching answers for this book, we were disturbed to find that many of the world's animals have rapidly declining populations and that this is almost always the result of human activity. Even when we're not hunting them to extinction for meat or sport, we're destroying huge chunks of their habitat. Enjoy them while you've got 'em, folks, because if we don't figure out a way to save them, they're going away forever.

So stay curious, don't feed the bears, and be kind to your web-footed (and all other!) friends. We'll see you around the Internet.

Just Curious about Animals and Nature,

Hey, Hey, We're THE Monkeys

"Here we come . . ." Tree-swinging, knuckle-dragging, and tool-using, some of us overdressed, others of us just oversexed. Our primate family tree has a whole barrel of monkeys swinging from it. No wonder "we get the funniest looks from everyone we meet."

The Family's Tree

Are gorillas a type of ape, or are apes gorillas?
Are monkeys and apes the same thing? Are humans
considered apes? Are simians different from primates?
Help, Jeeves, I'm so confused!

You're not alone, my anthropoid friend. Let's lay it out with a minimum of screeching, howling, and chest-beating:

Primates are human beings and all of the other animals that resemble us most closely. Primates have two main groups: *anthropoids* and *prosimians.*

1. **Anthropoids** include:

   Monkeys. New World monkeys live in South and Central America and include marmosets, tamarins, capuchins, howlers, spider monkeys, squirrel monkeys, woolly monkeys, and even woolly spider monkeys. Old World monkeys live in Asia and Africa and include baboons, colobus monkeys, guenons, langurs, and macaques.

   Apes. There are four major ape groupings–chimpanzees, gibbons, gorillas, and orangutans. Apes have no tails and are smarter than monkeys. Apes walk in an upright position instead of on four feet like monkeys. Apes actually climb trees; monkeys take a leap into them.

   Humans. It's pretty much just custom, religious dogma, and species egotism that keep people from proudly classifying themselves as apes. Most scientists don't make that distinction.

   By the way, if you exclude the humans from the above group, the apes and monkeys you have left are known as *simians.*

2. **Prosimians** include a number of lesser-known animals like aye-ayes, galagos, lemurs, lorises, pottos, and tarsiers. *Prosimii* means "premonkey"–in other words, they closely resemble the primitive primates that lived tens of millions of years ago before monkeys, apes, and humans began to evolve. Physically, prosimians have long, constantly wet noses like foxes instead of the flatter, drier noses of the anthropoids. Smell is more crucial to the prosimians, while anthropoids depend more on vision. Finally, the prosimians are not as strong or smart as the anthropoids.

   Not counting the lemurs, which are lucky enough to be isolated on the island of Madagascar, most of the prosimians have to directly compete for food with better-equipped monkeys and apes. In order to survive, prosimians became nocturnal hunters that scrounge for food while their larger, smarter cousins sleep.

Where can I learn more about prosimian primates?

Not So Smart Smart

What does Homo sapiens *mean?*

"Wise human." That's already a fairly ironic joke, considering. However, it gets better: because anthropologists have identified other ancient subspecies of *Homo sapiens* (for example, *Homo sapiens neandertalensis*), modern humans are now known as *Homo sapiens sapiens*. That, of course, means "wise wise human," which seems to be *really* overstating the matter.

What was the Neanderthal man named after?

The first fossils of our long-dead relative were discovered in 1856 in the Neander Thal ("Neander Valley") in Germany, so he became known as Neanderthal Man. The Neander Thal was named in honor of a minister and hymn writer, Joachim Neumann, who used to frequent the valley on nature walks in the late 17th century. So why didn't they call the valley Neumann Thal? Deciding to use a pseudonym for his hymns, Neumann (whose name means "new man" in German) translated his name into Greek and got Neander, which is the name by which he became well known. It became a strange coincidence that "New Man Valley" was named long before a new subspecies of man was discovered there.

Primate Colors

Do apes and monkeys see the same colors as humans?

Pretty much. Many of the New World monkeys are an exception to the rule–they don't see red that well, giving their world a blue, green, and gold hue.

Are they called orangutans because of their color?

No, it means "person of the forest" in the Malay language.

Gorilla Warfare

Are any apes as evil as some humans? Do they kill each other? Do they commit crimes against members of their own species?

In this regard, we'd have to confer with some of our closest relatives, the chimpanzees. Thanks to the work of researchers like Jane Goodall, we know a lot about chimpanzee behavior–both the best and the worst sort. And we do mean the very worst. Chimps have been known to murder other males while trying to gain dominance in a specific group. Lower-status males will sometimes steal food, sex, and other comforts while the dominant male isn't looking. And chimps commit rape. Of course, "rape" is a matter of definition, since normal chimp behavior often looks as if it's not that far removed from it. Dominant male chimps–twice as large as the females–often hold the power in sexual matters, regardless of what seem to be the females' preferences. Finally, chimps are very human in their capacity for war. They clash with other chimpanzee groups and will brutalize and kill their enemies.

On the other hand, under normal circumstances, chimpanzees have a great capacity for nurturing and being nurtured–with each other and with humans. Chimp mothers often adopt orphaned chimp babies and raise them as their own.

With such a complex range of behavior, chimpanzees are indeed very close cousins to humans. Alas.

Apes of Wrath

Do other primates besides people ever cannibalize each other?

Although the practice is uncommon, chimpanzees have been known to eat other chimps. To be fair, this only occurs under unusually dire circumstances like starvation–similar to times when humans have engaged in the practice. However, like some human groups, some chimps ritualistically eat the flesh of their dead opponents after a war. Biologists call this practice *anthropophagy* to reduce the emotional sting of the word *cannibalism.* We wouldn't want to stigmatize the dear little primates, after all.

Simian Meat Market

How many primates are major meat eaters?

Two: humans and chimps. You already know what people eat. A study of chimpanzee populations found that about 75 percent of the meat that chimps consumed consisted of red colobus monkey babies taken from their mothers. But researchers found that a chimp's main motivation for hunting is often sex—if members of a hunting party offer fresh meat to a female in heat, most or all are likely to get lucky.

The Other Side of the Family

If our closest relatives, the chimps, are naturally warlike, male-dominated, and violent, how can humanity have any hope of transcending its own worst traits?

Don't give up the ship, mate. Even if you believe that our natural selves cannot be completely transcended, we have another, gentler side of the family to look to for comfort.

Bonobos are a subspecies closely related to the chimps (in fact, they're sometimes called pygmy chimpanzees). Even though bonobos and chimps are our closest relatives, sharing 98.4 percent of our genes, the bonobos are not as familiar to us as the chimps, in part because they weren't even discovered by Westerners until 1929. Coincidentally, local natives along the Zaire River, where the bonobos live, have many myths about how humankind and bonobos were once brothers. (How close are bonobos to humans? That 98.4 percent genetic similarity makes them as close to us as a fox is to a dog.)

Bonobos and chimps are both believed to have split off from the same ancestors as humans not that long ago in evolutionary history—perhaps only 6.5 million years ago. Interestingly, unlike chimps and most other primates, the bonobos usually walk on two feet like humans, still affecting a hunched-over posture that closely resembles what scientists believe was the walking stance of our early human ancestors.

The bonobos give us hope by demonstrating that not all of our closest primate relatives are violent, warlike, cannibalistic, and exploitative. Instead, the bonobos are most interested in making love, not war. We can take comfort in the fact that some of them are lewd, obscene, and downright oversexed. In fact, they go at it like monkeys, as it were. Actually, much more often than monkeys–they've developed a female-led, cooperative, and fairly egalitarian society in which continuous and promiscuous sex has become a powerful substitute for aggression.

Compare what happens in a society of bonobos and in one composed of chimpanzees. If a group of chimps come upon food, the dominant male claims it as his own, using a display of aggression that ensures he gets a chance to eat his fill before allowing others to eat. On the other hand, a group of bonobos coming upon food will immediately get aroused and begin having sex–male and female, male and male, and (most common of all) female and female, all of them rubbing their genitals against those of another while grinning and making cooing sounds. After about five minutes, when all are feeling the magnanimous glow of orgasm, the bonobos go forward to feed as a community without regard to rank. Unlike chimps, bonobos don't hunt baby monkeys, or much of anything else, presumably since the guy bonobos don't have to do so to impress the gals. Except for an occasional small mammal, the bonobo diet contains very little animal protein.

A similar orgiastic thing happens when the bonobos come across anything that might be appealing enough to start conflicts. For example, when researchers in a zoo dropped a cardboard box into the compounds where chimps and bonobos lived, the dominant chimp used threats and violence to be the first to explore it. In contrast, the bonobos engaged in a brief orgy, and then all members of the group approached the box to explore it together.

Sometimes conflict happens anyway, despite the best-laid plans of the best-laid monkeys. For example, a bonobo adult might snap or hit at another peevishly. In that case, the matter is usually brought to a climax later by conciliatory activity that takes "kissing and making up" to whole new heights.

Perhaps corporate team-builders can find a lesson here somewhere.

Love Monkeys

Do any other apes except humans have monogamous and equal mating relationships?

Yes. Gibbons bond together as male and female and defend their territory from intruders, forsaking all others. All other apes, however, engage in some form of polygamy, wild sexual abandon, or both.

Do any primates other than humans have face-to-face sex?

Bonobos copulate face-to-face, looking deeply into each other's eyes. This occurs about a third of the time during sexual encounters. Humans once thought that they were unique in engaging in this especially intimate activity. In fact, Western scientists once believed that face-to-face sex was not even a natural position for humans but was a more advanced cultural innovation that had to be taught to primitive peoples (hence the term *missionary position*). Those clueless Western scientists were wrong on both counts.

Simian Says: Make a Rhyme!

Who was the gorilla from the Tom and Jerry *cartoons?*

Grape Ape.

Who was that cartoon gorilla with the hat, bow tie, and suspenders?

Magilla Gorilla.

What is the Latin name for the western lowland gorilla?

Gorilla gorilla gorilla.

Relative Humility

Who is more closely related: humans and gorillas, or gorillas and monkeys?

Humans and gorillas are closer relatives than gorillas and monkeys.

In The Blood of Rhesus

What does the Rh *in* Rh factor *stand for?*

Rhesus, as in the monkey that was once widely used in medical research. When Dr. Karl Landsteiner discovered some of the esoteric properties of blood in 1940, he decided to honor the rhesus monkeys that, in the process of making this discovery, were deprived of their freedom, blood, and lives.

Beware of Gorillas Making Hand Gestures

Does Koko the signing gorilla watch television?

She does. At some point, she went positively ape over *Mr. Rogers' Neighborhood.* Eventually Mr. Rogers came to visit Koko. Her response to seeing him in the flesh was interesting indeed, boys and girls: she wrapped her powerful arms around him, and then—as she had seen him do hundreds of times on TV—she reached down and took off his shoes.

Do signing gorillas use slang?

Well, maybe. Koko, the most adept signing gorilla ever, started using the sign for "nipple" for "people," perhaps because of the rhyme. She also started using "stink" for "flower." Another linguistic oddity she initiated is referring to any woman as "lips" and any man as "foot."

Can only gorillas use sign language, or have other apes been taught that too?

Chimps and, to a lesser extent, orangutans so far have also learned to sign. Washoe, the most accomplished chimpanzee, has a vocabulary of at least 240 words. He and his fellow chimps have so incorporated signing into their lives that they converse with each other by signing, and even "talk" to themselves when alone. While this chimp's vocabulary numbers are impressive, they're nowhere near the ones for Koko—her handlers say she can understand 2,000 spoken words and respond with a vocabulary of up to 1,000 signs. On the other hand, some of Koko's answers are so esoteric and random that sometimes you have to wonder how much of what she says is her intentional communication and how much is the interpretation of her trainers. For example, a transcript of an on-line chat revealed these questions and answers between Koko and her trainer, Dr. Penny Patterson:

Q: Are you going to have a baby in the future?
K: [signs] Inattention.
P: Oh, poor sweetheart, she said "inattention." She covered her face with her hands, which means it's not happening, basically, or "I don't see it."

Q: What do you want for your birthday?
K: Food smokes.
P: You have to understand that Smoky is the name of her kitten.

Q: Do you feel love from the humans who have raised you?
K: Lips apple give me.
P: People give her her favorite foods.

Where can I read transcripts of Koko the gorilla's on-line chats with fans?

Specs and Spans

How long are gorilla arms?

Gorilla arms are longer than their legs. Measured from fingertip to fingertip on outstretched arms, the longest span measured was nine feet, two inches. However, a more typical adult male arm span is about eight feet.

How much water does a gorilla typically drink in a day?

None. Gorillas get all the moisture they need from the leaves, tubers, flowers, fruit, fungus, and insects they eat—roughly fifty pounds of food a day.

Gorilla Warfare

Where did the name gorilla come from?

Calling some big hairy guy a gorilla isn't as much an interspecies insult as you would imagine (at least not to the person, although gorillas might have a different opinion). That's strange, because although we usually can safely assume that the animal had the name before we twisted it into a derogatory description of a human being, in the case of the gorilla, *people* had the name for nearly twenty-three centuries before it was applied to an ape.

Gorilla was first used by the Greeks in the 5th century B.C. They got the name from *Gorillai,* the name of a particularly hairy tribe of African natives. Greeks began using the word to describe any group of people they considered socially primitive. The British eventually picked it up and, in 1799, began using *gorilla* to mean any hairy aboriginal human. It wasn't until fifty years later that the term was used for a nonhuman. An American missionary named Thomas S. Savage was the first non-African to see a gorilla. In 1849 he gave it the name that had previously meant a hairy native person, and it stuck.

Does the word guerrilla have anything to do with gorilla?

No. *Guerrilla* means "little war" in Spanish.

What should you do if charged by a gorilla?

First of all, complain to your credit card company (okay, okay, so it's an old joke). . . . Being charged by a gorilla can be a very serious thing, so let us not digress any further. The good news is that gorillas are normally very shy and amiable; the bad news is that if you wander into their territory, the male leader will charge at you, beating his chest and looking mighty mean as the females and children run in the other direction. Gorillas may not have any natural enemies, but they're not real keen on trespassers.

So what do you do if a gorilla comes running at you, beating his chest and growling? You must, at all costs, *not* do the rational thing—run. Intruders who run away are often chased down and killed. Instead, screw up your courage, stand up straight, and hold your ground. Those who do are almost never harmed.

What happens when a silverback gorilla is defeated by another male?

All good things must come to an end. A typical gorilla band is led by one silverback male—a gorilla old enough that some of its back hair has turned gray. Traveling in his entourage are several mature females, one or two subordinate males, and young gorillas of both genders. Eventually, though, he gets old enough that he can no longer defend himself from interlopers from outside the group or even from his once-loyal subordinates. To the victor goes the harem and the perks of leadership, but what becomes of the vanquished silverback? Does he stick around and act as elder statesman and senior adviser?

No such luck. He is vanquished completely from the group. A silverback defeated by a rival will lead a solitary life from that day on.

Gorillas Will Be Missed

Are there any zoos in the U.S. that have mountain gorillas like those that Dian Fossey worked with?

There are fewer than 650 mountain gorillas left in the wild, and not a single one in zoos. It's difficult to transport mountain gorillas from their remote homes in central Africa. More significant, though, is that they don't survive well outside their native habitat. Unlike their common lowland cousins, and despite multiple attempts, no mountain gorilla has survived captivity for more than a few years.

Hopped-up Cappuccino Monkeys

Do capuchin monkeys have anything to do with cappuccino?

More than any reasonable person could expect. Both were reportedly named after the distinctive robe and cowl worn by Capuchin monks: the coffee drink because it's the same distinctive color, and the monkey because the dark brown hair on top of its head looks like a monk's hood. You may have seen capuchins in monkey suits (although you may have missed the tell-tale head markings, since they were wearing a hat)–they're the ones used by organ grinders to collect coins from passersby.

The Insouciance of Euro-Monkeys

Did wild monkeys ever live in Europe?

"Did"? They still do. Barbary apes live on the Rock of Gibraltar, a British colony at the gateway to the Mediterranean

Sea on the southern tip of Spain. Despite the name, this "ape" is really a monkey related to the rhesus monkey of India, and should probably be renamed, more accurately, the Barbary macaque.

The British government protects the monkeys on Gibraltar. Legend has it that the monkeys once returned the favor by warning the British of a sneak attack by the Spanish Armada. According to tradition, the British will always hold the rock as long as the monkeys live there.

There are only 5,000 Barbary apes worldwide, with the bulk of them living in remote areas of Morocco and Algeria, in northern Africa.

Sea Monkeys?

Can gorillas swim?

No. In case you're ever chased by one (which admittedly doesn't happen that often), face it down. Short of that, head toward the river; a gorilla won't follow you into the water. Some monkeys do swim, however–for example, the proboscis monkeys of Borneo are as graceful gliding through the water as they are swinging from the trees.

And God Said, Send in the Monkeys!

If people evolved from apes and monkeys, then why are apes and monkeys still around today?

This is most commonly asked by creationists–mostly well-meaning Christians who wish to hold up their Bibles as absolute and literal truth in the face of overwhelming evidence to the contrary.

Still, it's an intriguing question, because on the face of it, it sounds like it would sort of make sense: You have apes long ago that slowly get smarter and less hairy, eventually becoming humans with all of the benefits thereof (fast food, fast cars, fast Internet connections, etc.). If they evolved from a lower form (apes) to a higher and better form (humans), then you'd think the laws of evolution would ensure that all the members of the species would also change, right?

Well, in reality the question is a little like asking, "If I evolved from my great-grandfather Fred, how could it be that my cousin Bertha also evolved from him?"

The scientific evidence points to the conclusion that all primates evolved from some no-longer-existing common ancestor. What's interesting is that not all the primates split off at the same time into different groupings. Scientists believe that almost 7 million years ago, some early forms of gorilla split off from the chimps-and-humans line, and that a little over 6 million years ago, early human ancestors went a different direction from the early chimps. Since that time, scores of different species branched off from each of the lines. All of these species were like tree branches, the theory goes, splitting off in different directions, many of them living concurrently, some thriving, and some dying out. For example, in the same time as early modern humans–*Homo sapiens*–lived, at least three other peoplelike cousins also lived: *Homo erectus, Homo heidelbergensis,* and *Homo neandertalensis.* Also living, of course, were all of the other various cousins–the gorillas, the chimps, etc.

The different primates evolved in different ways to best adapt to the environmental conditions of the place and time in which they lived. Gorillas, chimps, and humans evolved with characteristics that made each best suited to their particular environment–whether plains, forest, or the urban jungle. No one species is necessarily higher or more advanced than another, just differently adapted.

So that's why there are still apes living alongside us. Wave hello to your cousins. They may have limited intelligence and lousy table manners, but that's often true of cousins in general, wouldn't you say?

When and why did the phrase "I'll be a monkey's uncle" become popular?

"I'll be a monkey's uncle!" was a socially acceptable substitution for the shockingly blasphemous phrase "I'll be damned!" It became popular around 1925 during the famous Scopes "Monkey Trial," in which Tennessee history teacher John Scopes was prosecuted and convicted for the crime of teaching about the theory of evolution.

***After John Scopes was found guilty of illegally teaching
about the theory of evolution, how long was it before
those laws were repealed in Tennessee?***

It was a crime to inform Tennessee schoolchildren that a theory
of evolution even *existed* until 1967. That was roughly forty-two
years after Scopes was prosecuted.

The Chimp Is Not My Son

Would chimpanzees make good house pets?

Not at all. Don't even think of it. For one thing, they can live
more than fifty years, which is quite a commitment. For
another, even a toddler chimp is stronger than you'll ever be,
and an adult can easily lift 600 pounds without straining much.
That might not necessarily be a problem, except that they grow
to be ornery as well. They generally refuse to acknowledge the
concept of toilet training, they're aggressive, they can never be
fully domesticated, and they enhance their status within their
tribe by constantly testing those above them to see if there's a
weakness somewhere. Even if you could establish that you and
your family were the alpha members of the tribe—as you can do
with a dog—it would not take long for your pet to realize that it
could easily whup all of you hairless primates upside the head
with one hand holding a banana.

But let's say you genuinely feel you can handle a baby chimp
and intend to return it to the jungle when it reaches adolescence.
Still—don't do it. Baby chimps don't stay children for long, and
returning one to the wild after raising it would be handing it a
death sentence. The other chimps in the wild are not in the habit
of accepting a new chimp into their midst, and they would likely
kill it if it tried to join their group. So keeping in mind the
example of Michael Jackson and Bubbles (below) and the fact
that the poaching of chimps for research labs and private
collectors is threatening their existence in the wild, it is best not
to monkey around with chimpanzees as house pets.

What happened to Michael Jackson's chimp, Bubbles?

Michael Jackson claimed he rescued Bubbles from a
cancer-research lab in Texas. For a few years the two cute little
primates were inseparable, and the chimp was pampered.
Bubbles reportedly had twenty matching designer outfits and

got his own hotel room when he traveled, and Jackson talked baby talk to him while changing the chimp's diapers. How precious.

However, the baby chimp grew up and became less cute and more unpredictable. He began challenging Jackson for the dominant male position, and Jackson had trouble holding his own in the competition. In 1988 Jackson claimed that Bubbles had slugged him, and after conferring with primate expert Jane Goodall, he gave his eleven-year-old chimp friend to a private zoo.

Still, We Wouldn't Trust Any of Them with No. 2 Pencils

If you gave animals an IQ test, which ones would be the smartest?

From various estimates of intelligence among animals, it's clear that primates rule in the smartness scale. Of the top ten, seven are in that category. (However, keep in mind that primates came up with the concept of being measured, so maybe you should take this ranking with a grain of salt.) Here's how they stack up:

1. Humans
2. Chimpanzees (including bonobos)
3. Gorillas
4. Orangutans
5. Baboons
6. Gibbons
7. Monkeys
8. Smaller toothed whales (especially the killer whale)
9. Dolphins
10. Elephants

How big is a chimpanzee's brain?

About half the size of a human's.

Marmoset There'd Be Days Like This

What is the smallest monkey?

The pygmy marmoset, which is about the size of a small squirrel and weighs about as much as a Quarter Pounder, bun and all. In fact, marmosets clamber up trees like squirrels–they're one of the few monkeys that have claws instead of finger- and toenails. While up in the trees, they feast on insects and fruit, and chew holes in trees to suck out the sap.

What's the loudest monkey?

The howler monkey. A small band can make as much noise as a stadium full of people and can be heard three miles away.

It seems like they'd be hard to catch—do any predators eat tree monkeys?

Eagles do, swooping down and grabbing them with their powerful talons. Still, they're better off than monkeys that spend a lot of time on the ground. All of the meat eaters from lions to hyenas seem to want rhesus pieces.

Cold Enough to Freeze a Brass Monkey

How can I put this delicately? I was watching some chimps at the zoo, and noticed that they seemed to have enormous testicles compared to male humans'. The gorilla next door had tiny ones. What gives?

Most people think that a gorilla would be hung like an ape, and they're surprised to find out that they're wrong. Despite being the largest primate, weighing in at 350 to 450 pounds, the gorilla has testicles that weigh only a bit more than 1 ounce total for the pair. Although humans and orangutans are lighter than gorillas, they are better endowed, weighing in at 1.5 ounces. What's even more surprising is that the 100-pound chimpanzee's testicles tip the scales at a whopping 4 ounces.

Biologists and insecure male humans have long puzzled over the mystery of why that might be. Finally, after a lot of research that involved invading the privacy of an awful lot of primates, they finally, once and for all, figured it out.

Not too surprisingly, it turns out that the size of a primate's testicles are a really good indicator of sperm count. What researchers didn't count on was that sperm count is a good indicator of how secure a male is in the love of a good female primate.

Females, although infinitely divine, are by nature notoriously fickle things. Females in species after species—primates and otherwise—hedge their reproductive bets by mating with whatever males they can find. This is good for them and the propagation of said species, because it ensures that their eggs get fertilized. However, what's good for them is profoundly unsettling to the males, who can never be sure that they are the real fathers of the children of their mates.

So what does this have to do with the size of ape testicles? Generally, the more promiscuous the women are within a species, the larger the testicles of the males who love them. Based on the same principle that buying more tickets ups your chance of winning the lottery, the males with the biggest testicles (and sperm counts) tend to have a better chance of reproducing with promiscuous females.

Given that, you can fairly accurately infer each species' sexual behavior by measuring the males' testicles. For example, male gorillas are pretty secure. They live in closed societies in which they constantly watch the females and make a point of running off any male interlopers. So gorillas can easily get by with small testicles and sperm counts to match—about 65 million of the little guys per ejaculation.

Chimpanzees, at the other extreme, mate promiscuously. A female chimp in heat will take on suitors left and right, and the males are equally ready to jump when the opportunity presents itself. The males with the highest sperm counts have competed best in the reproductive lottery that has continued over millions of years. As a result, those well-endowed chimps and other promiscuous male primates have testicles the size of cannonballs, and routinely issue forth billions of sperm with each ejaculation.

How do humans shape up in comparison, then? Someplace in between, considering our levels of both female fidelity and male fertility. An average human male sends off between 200 and 500 million sperm per ejaculation.

Interestingly, even among individual humans, the sperm levels are also somewhat dependent on how much security the male feels regarding the fidelity of his partner. Males in couples that spend most of their time together have lower sperm counts; yet the same males, when separated from their partners for more time, develop higher sperm counts, even when the interval between ejaculations remains constant. Interestingly, that same fact holds true in adulterous relationships, where time together is usually rare and irregular; as a result, a disproportionate number of children born to adulterous human females are sired by their lovers instead of their husbands.

Walk Like a Man

Does any ape or monkey normally walk on two legs only?
The gibbon does, holding its arms up and out for balance.

Do any apes or monkeys not live in forests or jungles?
Baboons are adapted to living on solid ground. They generally avoid forests, spend little time in trees, and are most comfortable traveling in herds on open land.

A Tail with a Happy Ending

What is "tail-twining"?
It's an affectionate practice of the tiny titi monkeys of the Amazon. Two, three, or four titis sit on a branch while resting or sleeping and wrap their tails together into a friendly, loving spiral.

Slithery Snakes
Slimy AND Toads

Reptiles and amphibians have freaked people out since the dawn of time. For example, the poor snake has been maligned since that whole Eve-and-the-fruit incident. It's patently unfair. And take frogs and toads: Most people won't touch 'em, but do they really cause warts? All in all, reptiles and amphibians may be slimy, scaly and ornery, but they're really cuddly on the inside. Read on. . . .

Here's a Hanky, Mr. Croc

What's with the expression crocodile tears? Do crocodiles really cry without meaning it?
Saltwater crocodiles shed tears often. Sea turtles and a number of seagoing birds do the same. It's

how they've adapted to drinking briny sea water–they shed the salt through their tear ducts, which desalinate the water they've slurped down.

Who was the first mugger?

Mugger is the name of a crocodile species that lives in India and Pakistan. The name got generalized to include human predators, as well.

It's Greek to Us

What does crocodile mean?

It comes from the ancient Greek *krokodilos,* meaning "worm of the pebbles." Why they thought this was a good name instead of something like "monster lizard of the water" is quite unclear.

The Art of Escape

If a crocodile is chasing you, I've heard you should run in a zigzag to confuse it. True?

Although the brain of a crocodile or alligator is quite small, zigzagging probably won't outsmart it. The most important thing to do if there's a huge reptile following you is put distance between you and the crocodilian (refers to both alligators and crocodiles). Logically, the fastest and easiest way to do this is by running straight ahead. Although alligators and crocs are capable of speeds up to 30 mph, they have no stamina whatsoever. Given a head start, a human can almost always outrun them–unless, of course, they're doing something stupid like zigzagging instead of running. The good news is that you'll probably never find yourself the object of a crocodile's pursuit. When an alligator or crocodile is moving fast, it's almost always trying to get away from a perceived threat, making a beeline for the safety of the water. They use the "surprise attack" method for getting food, as opposed to the "chase and conquer" method favored by lions or wolves. If you want to avoid crocodilians, stay away from the water's edge where they live, because they do occasionally lunge out of a swamp bank at lightning-fast speeds to consume an unsuspecting bird or deer.

By Hook or Croc

In J. M. Barrie's Peter Pan, *does Hook finally get eaten by the crocodile, or, as in the Disney version, does he exit leaving the reader guessing?*

In the book, the crocodile hooks his supper in the end. Seeing that he had been bested by Peter and overrun by all of the boys, Captain James Hook goes overboard to be consumed by the hungry crocodile. If only Disney would stop changing the true endings of classics—but we suppose they wanted to leave open the option for a *Peter Pan II: The Sequel.*

One's Salt, the Other's Fresh

What's the difference between crocodiles and alligators?

If you've encountered any crocodilian in Florida, chances are it's an American alligator. While American crocodiles do live in the salty, brackish waters of the southernmost tip of Florida, they are extremely secretive and almost never spotted in the wild. In contrast, alligators live in fresh water along riverbanks and in swamps, and aren't as elusive as rowers and campers might hope.

Physically, alligators have a broad, square snout. Crocodiles have a narrow snout and are more grayish green than their darker alligator cousins. Their most easily distinguished characteristic, however, is their teeth. Alligators have a pocket in their upper jaw that houses the bottom teeth when the jaw is shut. But crocodiles lack this space, and their teeth protrude from the sides of their mouths when shut.

Why You Rarely See Reptiles on *Jeopardy*

How big is an alligator's brain?

About as big as your thumb. But keep in mind that, in relation to body size it's one of the larger reptilian brains on Earth.

How do you make an alligator let go if it's chomping on your arm?

You might not be able to. Your best bet is a hard punch to the sensitive snout area, or a poke in the eye. Good luck!

Hot Boys, Cool Girls

Which parent determines the sex of alligator babies?

This is sort of strange: alligators, like many other reptiles, don't have sex chromosomes. As a result, gender isn't determined by the genes of the parents. Instead, whether Mama gator will be blessed with a baby girl or boy is completely decided by temperature.

When it's egg-laying time, the female finds a nice large area on the bank of her swamp, and digs a hole. She deposits her eggs–up to fifty–in the hole, and proceeds to cover them with leaf debris and mud, making a nest as large as six feet wide and three feet high. The soil and composting leaves provide the warmth the eggs need to mature. During the two-month incubation period, the mother stays in nearby waters to guard the nest.

Gender is determined during the second and third week of incubation. If the eggs are incubated at 86° F or below, the eggs will produce only females. If the eggs are incubated during this same period at 93° F or above, the offspring will be all male. If the eggs simmer at a more moderate 88°F, as most nests do, there will be a mix of both male and female babies.

At the end of incubation, the first mature alligator babies begin to make a barking noise from inside their shells. Barking alligators can be heard up to fifteen yards away, and this signals to Mom that it's hatching time. The mother's presence is crucial, as she is the one who uncovers the eggs from their buried home. If the mother isn't available or fails to hear the barking, the offspring can't hatch and will die.

No matter what gender emerges, mother alligators are very protective. For the first two years of life, babies travel with Mom–sometimes on her back or in her mouth–and she aggressively guards them from predators such as otters, turtles, skunks, raccoons, and even other alligators.

Pet Sounds

How loud is an alligator?

At its loudest–when it bellows–it's about as loud as a small plane. At a distance of sixteen feet, that measures about 92 decibels.

> What note do male alligators bellow to?
> B-flat.

> What do crocodiles and alligators sound like?
> **Ask**

See You Later, Masticator

Does an alligator chew its food?

Only to break the food up into pieces it can swallow. Although the alligator sports very strong jaws and teeth sharp enough to crush bones and other hard matter, it prefers prey it can swallow whole. Inside the alligator's belly are small pebbles it has swallowed that help grind up the food. What it can't swallow whole or break into smaller pieces, it will sometimes let sit and decay for a while until it can be broken up for consumption.

What's an alligator pear?

It's another name for an avocado.

Alleged Alligators

Is there any truth to the rumors that alligators live in the sewers of New York City?

Digging through a list of *New York Times* stories over the years will turn up a dozen instances in which alligators or crocodiles have mysteriously shown up in the New York City area (usually in Westchester County, for some reason). However, almost none of the stories has anything to do with sewers, and most or all of the reptiles have turned out to be lost pets.

The "alligators in New York" stories began back in 1932, when two boys started a folktale that lingers to this day in New York mythology. The two teenagers said that they pulled a two-foot-long dead alligator from a sewer drain in New York, and claimed that the Bronx River was filled with them. The stories hit the newspapers, and a citywide gator hunt ensued. However, upon further investigation, the dead alligator turned out to be a neighbor's pet crocodile that had escaped from its pen weeks before the story unfolded. Likewise, no gators were found in the Bronx River, and the reptile frenzy died down after the authorities called off the hunt.

Still, rumors of alligators in the sewers just won't die, and occasionally someone dumps a pet into a city waterway, feeding the rumors further (as happened in 2001 with a two-foot caiman that was dumped in Central Park's Harlem Meer). The New York City Bureau of Water and Sewer Operations gets a handful of inquiries about them each year. The bureau's standard response is that not one representative of Sewer Operations has ever seen an alligator in the city's sewers. The bureau is quick to point out that alligators–cold blooded, heat-loving animals that they are–wouldn't be able to survive the freezing temperatures, not to mention the bacteria that thrives in the sewer system. And the most convincing evidence according to the BWSO design chief is that if there were alligators in the sewers, labor union officials would've been quick to cite the toothy work hazards as reason for another pay hike for employees. That hasn't happened yet. Stay tuned.

Where can I read about claims of alligators in New York City sewers?

Did Teddy Roosevelt own a pet alligator?

Although the Roosevelt White House had a number of exotic and unusual pets, the alligator belonged to an earlier president, John Quincy Adams. Adams explained that he kept it around because he enjoyed "the spectacle of guests fleeing from the room in terror." His foreign policy was only slightly better.

How many groups of reptiles are there in the world?

There are only four main groups left: crocodilians, snakes and lizards, turtles and tortoises, and the tuataras–an old lizard form found in New Zealand. All of them run the risk of extinction due to human encroachment, and due to humans wanting to turn them into pets, food, and ornaments. Of these, the snakes are at greatest risk. In fact, snakes may be the most at-risk group for extinction of *all* vertebrates, not just reptiles.

Gross Anatomy

Don't lizards' tails grow back when they're broken off?

A few lizards have tails that can break off when predators attack, and then grow an extension back again (the new growth is cartilage, not bone like the original tail). While this may seem like a cool thing to show to the neighborhood gang of kids, this parlor trick comes at great cost to the lizard.

A lizard's tail is made up of vertebrae, much like our backbones. The tails, however, have specialized vertebrae with fine cracks below each joint where they fit together. Think of those fine lines as dotted lines on tear-away coupons. The muscles surrounding these dotted-line areas are thin and can be easily torn without causing significant damage to the muscle fiber around them. Many lizards will frantically wiggle their tails when in danger, hoping predators will grab that end instead of their heads or bodies which would cause immediate death. Some lizards' tails are even brightly colored, to add to their attractiveness.

If a predator (including those of the curious-fifth-grader variety) grabs the wriggling tail, the tail will snap off where the bone and muscle are weak, and the lizard may escape. It's an amazing act of nature—but, as mentioned, it costs the lizard dearly. Some die later from the trauma. Also, the energy required to heal the wounds and grow the cartilage might be better used to last through a food shortage or some other natural catastrophe.

Do the suction cups on lizards' feet ever lose their suction, sending the lizards plummeting to the ground?

The lizards that climb walls and ceilings don't tend to fall off. But it's not because they have great suction—as a matter of fact, they're not really using suction at all.

Here's how the feet work: on the bottom are dozens and dozens of tiny grooves, which you can see if you've ever looked closely at a lizard in a glass-walled terrarium. On each of those little grooves you can see, there are dozens more that aren't visible to the naked eye. And on each of those dozens of grooves are hundreds, if not thousands, of hairlike bumps.

Now, if you take a microscopic look at even the smoothest of surfaces, you'll see it is covered with microscopic pits, bumps, and grooves. To a lizard, glass, tile, concrete, and sheet rock all offer plenty to hang on to. Its pads will grab and hang on, even if the lizard is scared, tired, sick, or dying. Sometimes it takes hours for a dead lizard to drop, because the feet are still clinging onto those tiny imperfections. While this is rare because most wall-climbing lizards tend to go hide somewhere level when they're sick, you still might want to keep a wary eye for falling lizards overhead.

Snake a Leg There, Buckaroo

How come snakes don't have legs?

Once, long ago in the course of their evolution, snakes had legs; they are actually descended from the same family as lizards. However, they gradually lost their legs as it became more efficient for them, in terms of energy conservation, to slither. Some primitive snakes, like the boa constrictor and the python, still have remnants of their legs, called *spurs*. These don't serve any purpose in locomotion, but–yippee-i-o-ki-ay!–they sure tickle the ladies. We mean that literally–they're sometimes used by male snakes to stimulate female snakes during courtship and mating.

Besides snakes, are there any other reptiles without legs?
A group of legless lizards erroneously called glass snakes lives in grassy and forested areas all over the world. Although they are called snakes, and even look like snakes with ears, if you pick them up, their bodies are much more rigid, like lizards, than bendable, like snakes. By the way, they get the "glass" part of their name because their long tails break off easily. But please don't attempt this (see page 24).

It Ain't Water into Wine, but It'll Do

Why is the basilisk sometimes called the Jesus Christ lizard?
In all seriousness, the basilisk lizard got its nickname because it can walk on water. Its feet are webbed just enough that when it's running at fast speeds, the lizard can skate above the water line. If the other lizards had sufficient faith, perhaps they could do it, too.

What Has Pits but No Arms?

Does a pit viper live in pits?
It's actually just another name for the common rattlesnake, which has highly sensitive pits located between its eyes and nostrils. These pick up even minute changes in temperature, so that the snake's ability to locate prey is very good. *Viper* is just a shortened version of *Viperidae,* the scientific name for the family of poisonous snakes that includes both the rattler and the European adder.

What exactly rattles when a rattler's rattle rattles?
There are not, as many people believe, tiny pebbles or other

What do rattlesnake rattles look like?

rattling things inside the snake's tail. A baby rattlesnake is born with a tiny, keratin-based hard shell at the end of its tail. Every time the baby sheds its skin, a new shell–slightly bigger–appears below, loosely attached to the one before it. When a rattlesnake shakes its tail, the rattles hit against one another, making the classic rattlesnake noise that scares away predators.

It was once believed that the number of rattles on a rattlesnake told its age. We now know this isn't true. Although the snake does add a rattle every time it sheds its skin, the snake molts between two and four times a year, so you can't get an accurate measure. Besides, wild snakes often end up breaking off rattles through normal wear and tear. So if you want their true age, better check some ID.

Are rattlesnakes edible?
Yes. Check out recipes at http://www.exoticmeats.com/recipes/079.asp.

Come Right Up & Whisper in My Mouth

Where are a snake's ears?

Snakes don't have ears. They "hear" by being close to the ground, and feeling vibrations move up through their bones. Other than that, their main method of gleaning information from the world around them is by smelling with their tongues. The tongue darts out, picks up chemicals and other environmental indicators, and then brings them back into the snake's mouth, where they're deposited on an organ in the roof of the mouth. This organ–called the Jacobson's organ–can detect even the tiniest of changes in the air, helping the snake to sense danger and locate supper.

Working for Scale

What's the name of the instrument that snake charmers use?

It's called a *pungi*–a generic term for several Indian reed instruments.

How do snake charmers get king cobras to dance to their rhythms?

It's a pretty impressive act. From the cobra basket, the snake rises as the crowd shrinks back. The charmer plays his *pungi,* swaying to the music, and the snake undulates with him, seemingly entranced. The crowd, equally mesmerized, throws coins into the snake charmer's basket.

Like other street performers with a good act, however, there's a catch. As mentioned above, snakes don't have ears, so there's no way a cobra can even hear the song that's being played. What happens is this: When the snake charmer takes the lid off the basket, the snake is thrust from darkness into light and rises up defensively, as it would in any threatening situation, fanning its hood. The snake charmer begins to play his pungi, swinging the end in front of the snake. The cobra mistakes the moving end of the instrument for another snake. Because a snake's eyes can't pivot, the cobra physically moves to follow the thing it's trying to strike at. Since the pipe is moving to a musical rhythm, it looks as though the snake is dancing. Experienced snake charmers know the distance and movements needed to keep the cobra following without lashing out. But just in case, many of these snakes have been defanged–a little tidbit most charmers don't tell you before taking your money.

Warning: You Could Be That Ninth of a Person

What are my chances of dying if I'm bitten by a poisonous snake?

Out of every 10 million people, only 2.9 will die from snakebites. That's roughly a 1 in 3,448,276 chance.

What Life Has Tortoise

What reptile is known to live the longest?

As far as we know, the turtles and tortoises live longer than any reptile, or any other animal, for that matter. An adult turtle found on the island of Mauritius in 1766 by the French explorer Marion de Fresne lived for another 152 years. Since the turtle was thought to have already been in its late twenties when it was found, it may have been as old as 180 at its death. Although this is an extreme case, it's fairly common for these shelled creatures to hit the ripe old age of 150.

They look the same, only different sizes. Are the turtles in our local park's pond closely related to the little pet turtles of my childhood, Tim and Jim?

More than likely it's the same species–the red-eared terrapin. Those kept as pets usually never reach maturity and die while still young, due to poor environment and nutrition. The ones in your local pond are full-grown adults, who may live as long as fifty to seventy-five years, and who may have been pets that people set free decades ago. When salmonella was recognized as a significant threat to pet terrapin owners, the U.S. Food and Drug Administration banned the sale of most pet turtles in 1975. Before that, though, you could buy baby turtles in pet stores, department stores, and even drugstores.

In Stinked

What makes the stinkpot turtle smell so bad?

Like the skunk, the stinkpot, and other turtles in the musk turtle family, have musk glands located on the fronts of their legs. If scared, they will release foul-smelling musk as a defense. While they're not uncommon, you just don't see them very often. When they emerge from the murky stream bottoms they so enjoy, it's usually at night to feed, and then back they go into the waters from whence they came.

The Voice of the Turtle

Where does the name turtle *come from?*

From the Latin *tortuca,* by way of the French word *tortue,* both meaning "tortoise."

What's the difference between tortoises and turtles?

Tortoises are land-dwelling turtles.

Where does the turtledove get its name?

From the Latin *turtur,* referring to the soft, cuddly, cooing noises the bird makes. Until recently, however, the turtledove was simply called a turtle, although it had nothing to do with the shelled amphibian. Now that confusing Bible verse makes sense: "The time of the singing of birds is come, and the voice of the turtle is heard in our land" (Song of Solomon 2:12).

I Led Two Lives

What does amphibian *mean?*

"Double life" in Greek, referring to the fact that these creatures are both land and aquatic dwellers during the course of their lives.

Not a Lizard or a GOP House Leader

Is a newt a salamander? What's the difference?

Yes, a newt is a type of salamander, meaning its skin is thin, and it breathes through gills until its lungs grow and it can leave the water. Newts are lizardlike, sporting a tail and four legs. Their legs, like those of many other salamanders, are weak in comparison to those of lizards, and are better equipped for aquatic than land locomotion. The biggest difference between newts and salamanders is that adult newts have flatter tails than salamanders. This isn't a big difference, we know, but it will have to do.

When a newt, equipped with a working set of lungs, finally leaves the water for a life on land, it's then called an *eft*. From then on, it will return to the water only to mate. Adult newts are brightly colored and are poisonous to predators. We can only guess that this is why "eye of newt" is part of the witches' recipe in act IV of Shakespeare's *Macbeth* ("Double, double toil and trouble; Fire burn and cauldron bubble").

Do some salamanders have gills?

Most salamanders have gills during their larval stage. They live in water and, like fish, breathe underwater. As they reach maturity (which can take years in some species), they lose the gills, develop lungs, and leave the water. But some types of salamanders never mature and live their entire lives in the larval stage. They keep their gills, stay in water, and breed there, without ever physically taking on adult characteristics like tougher skin and lungs. Some of these salamanders, like the axolotl, stay in their larval stage because important growth chemicals like iodine are missing from their watery environments. However, some cave-dwelling salamanders remain in their young forms regardless of outside influences. We know some people like that as well.

Kiss It and Find Out

What's the difference between a frog and a toad?

Toads don't spend as much time in the water as frogs do. As a result, their skin is thicker and retains moisture better, and they tend to be stockier in build than most frogs.

Is it true that toads will give me warts?

Warts in humans come from an internal virus that some of us carry and some of us don't. Warts can't be contracted or passed along by touching any amphibian. Although picking up a toad can be harmful to the toad (and it's likely to pee on you), it won't hurt you.

Frog in Your Throat?

Is the British dish "toad-in-the-hole" made of frog legs or other amphibian parts?

No, it's similar to the American dish "pig-in-a-blanket": sausages are dipped in batter, then baked. The origin of the name is not completely clear. The dish itself is at least 250 years old and probably older.

What do frog legs taste like?

Like chicken with a tad of fishiness thrown in for good measure. Think of it as "chicken of the swamp."

> What was the emblem on Catherine the Great's tableware?
> A frog.

What is a Toad Suck?

It's the name of a dam in Conway, Arkansas. Legend has it that back in the 1800s, river men were regulars at a saloon near the ferryboat landing, and local lore had it that these men would suck so much from the liquor bottle that they would swell up like toads. Today, Toad Suck is a nice family place, complete with a picnic area. It's also the site of the annual Toad Suck Daze, a festival that includes arts, crafts, music, expositions, and of course a toad-jumping contest. For more information about the festival (and entry rules if you want your toad to compete), see http://www.americaslibrary.gov/pages/es_ar_toad_1.html.

How come frogs blink when they swallow?

Because frogs don't have teeth and blinking helps them get their food down. This may not sound like an explanation on the face of it, but it is. Here's how: a frog's eyes, not unlike those of a hippopotamus, are bulgy, big, and located on the top of its head. This helps it to see even when the rest of its body is submerged in water. It also means that the area inside the body that houses these big eyeballs has to be large. When the frog swallows, it closes its eyes and pushes them down into their cavities, which are located at the back of the frog's mouth. This movement helps to push the wiggling bug down its throat. Since the frog's tongue is better designed to shoot out and retrieve food than push it down into its stomach, this system isn't a bad one. And frankly, if we had to eat bugs, we'd probably close our eyes, too.

Do frogs drink?

Not with their mouths. Like all other amphibians, frogs have naked skin–lacking hair, scales, and feathers–making it perfectly suitable for absorbing water. Their skin soaks up what they need, then filters it out through their kidneys, like the rest of us. Some toads don't even need actual water–they have a specialized patch called a seat in their bottoms that can absorb up to three-quarters of all their water needs while they sit in moist soil.

Not Legally Allowed in Toad Suck

How do South American hunters get the poison from poison arrow frogs without killing themselves?

Although the poison is in the mucus that the frogs secrete onto their skins, human skin can't pass the poison into the bloodstream through touch alone. However, if the person has cuts or abrasions or accidentally rubs his mouth or nose after touching a frog, he might become ill or die. Some of these frogs are so lethal–with enough poison in one frog to kill eight humans–that many South American hunters would rather not run the risk of accidental ingestion. When extracting poison, they will often simply skewer the frog into the ground with a stick while they coat their sharp darts with its sticky slime. For slightly less poisonous frogs, they capture them, skewer them, and roast them over a fire, collecting the drippings to use on their darts. What's even more dangerous than the actual collection of the poison is toting the darts on a hunt. If the sharp end of a dart accidentally goes into a man's skin, that's pretty much the end of the hunt for him. Happy trails, amigo!

Life's Roughage

They're symbols of love, beauty, and tranquillity. Plants are the source of medicinal and spiritual healing. They're also the cause of scratches, hives, and sometimes painful death. What evil lurks in the hearts of plants? Step into the dark side of the forest and we'll show you.

You Can Catch More Flies with Stinking Putrid Flesh

Why do some flowers smell like rotting meat?

One man's meat is another man's poison, as the old saying goes, and some flowers put this theory to the test. *Carrion flower* is the name given to several different species of plants, usually members of the lily family, that all use the same process for pollination–a gross, stinky smell. Flies and carrion beetles are attracted to them and get caught inside the flowers long enough to get coated with pollen, escape and, with any luck, go and pollinate another carrion flower. In 1993 David Attenborough, filming the BBC series *The Secret Life of Plants,* trudged into the depths of Indonesia's jungles to gather seeds from the endangered corpse plant, a foul-smelling flowering plant indigenous to Sumatra. The seeds were distributed to various universities and botanists, and in the summer of 2001 many of these plants flowered for the first time, causing a ripple of excitement through many botanists' hearts. The smell emitted for the 48 to 72 hours that the blooms remain open has been likened to cabbage soup, an overly hot greenhouse, manure, and of course, a rotting corpse. Ironically, the Indonesians use them as an aphrodisiac.

> Where can I see pictures of the corpse flower?

Plant Eating Man

Are there any plants that eat animals like in Little Shop of Horrors?

Well, yes. Carnivorous plants that eat insects have also been known, on rare occasions, to eat tiny amphibians and baby fish that inadvertently land within their jaws. However, if you're looking for a giant plant that eats big mammals or something, I'm afraid you'll have to stick to the shelves at your local video store.

How do carnivorous plants catch bugs?

In the same way that flowers attract bees: with color and smell. However, a carnivorous plant also has a mechanism that traps the bug once it lands. In the case of the pitcher plant, all varieties sport a hollow tube or bowl that has downward-sloping hairs on the inside and a lid on top. Digestive juices sit in the bottom of the bowl. An insect drawn to the plant, looking to get a little bit of nectar, goes into the hollow tube and can't get out because the hairs and lid make it difficult. It eventually flounders and drowns in the liquid at the bottom. Surprisingly, though, many of the bugs that fall into a pitcher plant do escape. Some insect species are completely immune to the digestive juices and actually set up house in the bottom of the plant, feeding on the other bugs that fall prey. Any leftover bug parts or the excrement of the living bug are still food for the pitcher plant, so everyone's happy—except, of course, the hapless bug victim.

In the case of the Venus' flytrap, the process is a little more complicated. The plant has triggers and moving parts that are necessary for it to catch insects. Without tendons or muscles, it's hard to fathom how exactly the plant does this, although we do know it involves a series of electrical impulses and may include the shifting of fluids within the plant's veins. Regardless, carnivorous plants are some of the more fascinating—and merciless—members of the plant kingdom.

Why do carnivorous plants eat insects? Why don't they get their food from the soil like other plants?

Carnivorous plants do get nutrients from the soil and air. However, carnivorous plants live in boggy areas where the soil lacks many nutrients that most plants need to survive. Bug supplements make it possible for these plants to live in their natural habitat.

Peach Pitfalls

Is it true that peach pits are poisonous?

Yes. When ingested, peach pits release what's called hydrogen cyanide—a gas that, in enough quantity, will kill you. Fresh almonds also release hydrogen cyanide gas when digested. Inadvertent cyanide poisoning happens periodically in countries like Turkey where fresh almonds are regularly eaten (roasting eliminates this danger, by the way). Other pits to avoid: cherries, plums, apricots, apples, and crabapples.

What product was it that was supposedly spiked with cyanide in the early 1980s?

There's no supposed about it. Potassium cyanide, a lethal cyanide-based chemical found in photographic darkrooms, among other places, was placed inside Tylenol capsules in and around the Chicago area in 1982. Seven people were murdered, and the culprit was never found. In 1986 a woman in Seattle, Washington, after a failed attempt to kill her husband with poisonous foxglove seeds, fed him four potassium cyanide-laced Excedrin, which did him in completely. When she was unsuccessful in collecting all of his life insurance policy, she laced a few more Excedrin bottles to cover her tracks and placed them on Seattle drugstore shelves, resulting in the death of one woman. Three more tainted bottles were found in the area and removed from the shelves before anyone else was poisoned.

The result of these two incidents was tamperproof packaging that keeps predators–and often us, ourselves–out.

Planning a Foe Garden

I have a two-year-old and want to grow a baby-safe garden. What plants should I stay away from that could poison my son?

More than you can imagine. Here's a partial list:

- **Rhubarb**—the leaves are fatal. Even cooked, they've been known to kill.
- **Buttercups**—all of these plants can cause damage to the stomach and intestines.
- **Oleander**—the leaves and branches are extremely poisonous. They act as a heart palpitation drug and can cause death.
- **Foxglove**—the leaves can be fatal.
- **Daffodils, narcissus, and hyacinth**—the bulbs are poisonous and may be fatal.
- **Azalea, laurel, and rhododendron**—all of these plants are highly toxic and can kill.
- **Jasmine**—the berries are fatal.
- **Iris**—the stems that grow underground can cause damage to the stomach and intestines.
- **Lily of the valley**—the flowers and leaves cause irregular palpitations of the heart.
- **Mistletoe**—the berries are fatal.
- **Oak**—the leaves and acorns can gradually poison, though it takes large quantities to do significant damage.
- **Cherry**—the limbs and leaves are fatal.
- **Daphne**—the berries are fatal.
- **Wisteria**—the seeds and pods are a common cause of child poisonings. They cause stomach and intestinal distress.

- **Castor bean**—the seeds can kill.
- **Elderberry**—all parts cause digestive distress.
- **Larkspur**—the seedlings and seeds act on the nervous system and can be fatal.
- **Monkshood**—the roots cause upset stomach and diarrhea and sometimes nervousness.
- **Autumn crocus and star-of-Bethlehem**—the bulbs induce vomiting.
- **Bleeding heart**—the leaves and roots, if eaten in large amounts, may be fatal.
- **Elephant ear**—the whole plant can cause intense allergic reaction if ingested and has led to anaphalactic shock.
- **Yew**—the berries and leaves are fatal. No symptoms accompany this poisoning, just death.
- **Jack-in-the-pulpit**—all parts cause burning when ingested.
- **Nightshade**—all parts are fatal.
- **Poison hemlock**—this plant resembles a carrot, and all parts of it are deadly.

Well, you get the idea. Ultimately, if you truly want a safe garden, it needs to start with your child. Don't leave him unattended, and teach him not to put anything in his mouth. Perhaps you should consider a vegetable and herb garden (although beware–even some of these plants have toxic parts).

Talk to your pediatrician and your local nursery (the green variety) for a complete list of safe plants.

Bad Sporesmanship

What nutritional value does a mushroom have, exactly?
A lot, but not enough to risk eating one in the wild, for sure, especially if you don't know what you're doing. Identifying mushrooms is extremely difficult even for the experienced. Store-bought mushrooms are a good source of several vital nutrients, including magnesium, potassium, phosphorus, and selenium. They're also high in fiber. But then again, out in the wilds, so is a piece of pine bark. Stick with that in an emergency, and you run no risk of poisoning. (Our advice? Look but don't touch.)

> Where can I get a field guide to mushrooms?

Why are mushrooms called toadstools?

Not all are—only the ones that'll kill you. And that's where the name comes from. The German word for poisonous mushrooms is *todesstuhl,* meaning "death's stool." English speakers heard "toad stool," and this botched translation stuck. Since many mushrooms do resemble little chairs, it wasn't too hard to imagine little forest toads taking a quick sit-down on one of them on their way through the woods.

Which mushroom is the aphrodisiac?

There's no specific one that we could find, just an old adage about mushrooms in general being aphrodisiacs. Although many people say they find their shapes and textures erotic and sensual, there's no evidence whatsoever that mushrooms contain anything that would incite lust upon consumption. As a matter of fact, while researching this, we ran across several website bulletin boards where women were discussing this very issue. One woman in particular advised that when potential partners try this tired, worn-out recipe for love on her, it has the exact *opposite* effect and sends her running (she *hates* mushrooms). Consider this, boys, as you plan the menu for your next date.

Have mushrooms always been a delicacy enjoyed by rich folks, or is this just another faddish status symbol of today?

Despite their instant availability to rich and poor alike, mushrooms have long been considered the food of kings. Consider the historical prominence the mushroom has enjoyed on the dinner table of the rich and powerful: in ancient Egypt, mushrooms were considered such a delicacy that only pharaohs were allowed to eat them. And remember ancient Roman emperor Claudius, who was the worthy and crippled ruler of Rome? He was quite fond of fungus—so much so that it finally did him in. His fourth wife (and the mother of Nero), Agrippina, was so intent upon placing her son on the throne that she succeeded in murdering Claudius by feeding him a potently poisonous variety, masquerading the lethal mushroom as his old stand-by. After twelve hours of speechless gagging, Claudius finally kicked the bucket, and Nero was crowned.

I know mushrooms aren't in the plant family, really, but they're very closely related to plants, aren't they?

Well, yes, sort of. Fungi are not animals, for sure. Like plants, they do have a root system and also bloom (the mushroom itself is the bloom) for reproductive purposes. But mushrooms lack the green chlorophyll that's absolutely essential for true plants to create food for themselves. An argument could be made (and it has) that mushrooms behave more like insects than plants. It's the function of fungi to break down plant matter in the soil, much as ants, worms, and larva do. Not only is fungi found on trees, leaves, and other dead material on the forest floor, but it can also be found along walls and in foods–anything that's capable of rotting. The mushroom simply couldn't be boxed in to any one category, so the kingdom of Fungi had to be created to describe these organisms.

Ears Lookin' at You, Kid

Where does the word smutty *come from?*

From pure-hearted farmers. *Smut* is the name of a mold that grows in corn ears. The mold breaks off into fine dirtlike powder when the corn is shucked; therefore the word *smut* became synonymous with *dirt,* or *dirty.* When *dirty* came to describe sexual talk or writing, calling the same behavior "smutty" seemed to make it even more reviled.

Wild Sex in the Garden

Are all flowers both sexes—male and female—and capable of playing either role in reproduction?

No. Here's a quick flower primer: There are actually three types of flowers. The "perfect" flower, which is what you're familiar with when it comes to plant reproduction, is the first type. It has male and female reproductive organs, and both are functional. Pollen from the stamen makes its way to the pistil of another flower, and reproduction occurs. The second type of flower is also called "perfect," but it has a glitch. There are both male and female parts, but only one participates in reproduction. For instance, one may have a stamen (male), but only the pistil (female) is functional in reproduction; other flowers in the same bed will be the reverse–both parts are present, but only the stamen works. Sunflowers fall into this category, as well as many other ornamental flowers with large, showy blooms. Finally, there's what's called the "imperfect" flower. It has only the male or female reproductive part, not both. Many trees' flowers belong to this group. The problem with imperfect flowers is that only the female flowers produce fruit or seeds; a plant with only male flowers is barren. Still, breeders have been able to work with imperfect flower plants such as cucumbers, creating hybrids that have an abundance of fruit-producing female flowers and only a couple of male flowers on each plant.

She Comes on Like a Rose

Is there any good reason for the existence of poison ivy besides being the incessant pest of gardeners, hikers, and children?

Considering how violent some reactions to its oils can be, it's hard to imagine poison ivy serving any good purpose. The English colonist John Smith, in 1609, wrote home about his run-in with this dreaded toxic plant: "The poisonous weed, being in shape, but very little different, from our English Yvie; but being touched causeth reddness, itchinge and lastly blysters, the which however after a while they pass away of themselves with out further harme."

Despite the misery it causes, poison ivy does have significant wildlife value, most importantly as a food source. Many small animals and deer are not allergic to it and consume all parts of the plant—leaves, berries, and twigs. Birds depend on poison ivy berries during the fall and winter months when food is scarce. Furthermore, this plant is very adaptable and can grow as a bush or a vine. Insects use the woody vines as pathways and protective structures up and down trees, and small animals can seek shelter under poison ivy in its bush form. For these reasons, wildlife groups will never weed it out of state parks and national forests. That means it's up to you to know how to identify poison ivy so you can protect yourself from it.

Besides taking precautions with clothing, and staying on hiking paths, it's best to know what you're looking for so you don't stumble into it inadvertently. Poison ivy is a crafty little plant that can grow in several different incarnations. It can look like groundcover, a vine, or a shrub. It often grows along and over fences with other rambling weeds. The leaves can be smooth and waxy, or they can be dull and rough-textured, with jagged edges. They can grow up to ten inches in length, or they can be as small as an inch or two. The leaves are red in autumn and when they are young, but they're green through the summer. As you can see, it can be a very confusing plant to identify. But here's something to look out for: all poison ivy, no matter the leaf size or color, has three leaves per stem. Two of the leaves are opposite one another and growing in different directions. One leaf is at the top and has a longer stem than the two side leaves. Remember the old adage, "Leaves of three, let them be," and leave the playing in poison ivy to the wildlife.

How long does it take for a rash to appear after contact with poison ivy?

In general, it takes anywhere from twelve to forty-eight hours. The rash can hang around, though, itching like crazy, for ten miserable days or up to two unbearable weeks.

Is poison ivy a member of the regular ivy family? Can our English ivy cross-pollinate with the poison variety?

No, they belong to two separate plant families, despite the similar name. English ivy belongs to the ginseng family and is considered true ivy. As nutty as this may seem, poison ivy is a member of the edible cashew family. The shells of the cashew nut also contain oils that can cause an allergic reaction, as do the rind of the mango and the ginkgo tree—two other members of this same family.

Another odd classification is kudzu, the out-of-control Japanese groundcover that has taken over the southern United States. It's not an ivy, either, despite some visual similarities. It's a member of the pea family.

Features from the Black Legume

Who wrote, "Beans, beans, they're good for your heart. The more you eat, the more you fart"? And do beans really make you fart, anyway?

No one person has claimed rights to this literary gem. Some time in the 1600s, though, people began creating haughty, naughty little rhyming couplets to place on lavatory and brothel walls instead of the usual "Ivon woz 'ere," and "Georgina's my gal." Believe it or not, the "Beans, beans" poem originated from this seventeenth-century collection of graffiti. Like any oral history, it has changed form over the years into the rhyme every nine-year-old school kid knows and loves today. There are many variations, but here's a common one:

> Beans, beans, they're good for your heart,
> The more you eat, the more you fart.
> The more you fart, the better you feel,
> So eat those beans at every meal.

And beans'll definitely make you break wind. They contain certain sugars called oligosaccharides that have a large molecular structure. In plain English that means they don't get digested very well in the small intestine, leaving lots of chunks for colonies of bacteria to chow down on. (Fruits, whole grains, and vegetables do the same thing.) The bacteria in the intestines multiply when they have a lot to eat, and this process produces gas. The gas has to go somewhere (out) or you'll explode like a cockroach–and that would just be gross.

They can make soybeans taste (sort of) like meat, cheese and milk. What else can they make from soybeans?

Animal feed, oils that go into ice cream, soap, explosives, salad dressing, biodegradable plastic, adhesive, diesel fuel, paint, linoleum, ink, cosmetics, faux leather, and a whole lot more. Henry Ford was so enamored of the soybean that he tried to make an all-vegetable car in the 1930s, and was the first to install soybean plastic on all the knobs in his cars, soybean fiber in the seat cushions, and soybean oil in the enamel paint. Thanks to Ford, a true soy pioneer, many cars today still sport soy gearshifts and the like.

They appear to be too closely related to be separate vegetables, so why are black-eyed peas called peas, while navy beans or pinto beans are called beans?

They're very closely related in that they're all *legumes,* a group of plants that are nutritionally beneficial to humans. Legumes (Latin for "seedpods") include clover, alfalfa, mimosas, rosewood, indigo, peanuts, beans, and peas. All of these plants share the unique ability to glean nitrogen from the air around them, instead of strictly through their root systems like other plants. That makes them economically valuable to farmers.

Although some peas look like beans and vice versa, and both groups have what's called "pea-shaped" flowers, a couple of distinguishing characteristics generally separate these plants. Peas are cool-weather plants, whereas beans grow best with heat. Peas also have clinging tendrils that creep out and wrap around things as they grow. Beans, on the other hand, act like a true vine–the whole stem of the plant wraps around things as it grows. In general, peas are picked green and early and are taken from the pod to eat, while beans usually ripen in the pod (this is what produces what we call "dried beans"). Only a few types of beans are eaten within the pod–the familiar snap beans and wax beans, to name two.

Show Me Your Peanuts

What part of the world grows the most peanuts?

India. China's second. Believe it or not, the U.S. grows less than 10 percent of the world's peanut supply. However, as you'd suspect, most U.S. peanuts are grown in Alabama and Georgia.

Where do peanuts originate?

Originally, peanuts were grown in South America. South American Indians were cultivating the peanut over a thousand years before European settlers arrived in North America.

Man Eating Plant

Can you live by just eating grass if you had to?

Maybe longer than you'd live if you had nothing to eat, but grass–along with most other plant material, besides legumes– can't sustain a human for very long without other nutrients in the diet. Why? Because humans can't digest plant matter very well, and we only get one shot at it: plants go in, get digested as much as possible, and the roughage pushes through.

One of the reasons grass works well for cows, horses, guinea pigs, and other ruminants is that they have a system of redigesting the stuff. Cows regurgitate grass, ruminate, and swallow again, giving the grass extra chances to break down. Instead of regurgitation, a guinea pig actually has a pouch near the anus where poop is stored. When the poop still contains undigested and valuable food particles, the guinea pig chews on the poop a while, swallows, and lets it all digest again. Considering these alternatives, it seems humans have made out pretty well. . . .

Seduction . . . or Canola?

How did Canola oil get its name?

The name Canola came from blending the two words *Canada* and *oil.* Canola oil hit the U.S. marketplace in 1986, but in places like Europe, India, and China, this healthy and low-fat oil has been used for centuries, and known as rape oil. The rape plant (*rape* means "turnip" in Latin) is a member of the mustard family, as are cabbage, turnip, and horseradish. While other oils are named after the plants they come from—peanut oil, olive oil, corn oil, and safflower oil, for instance—rape oil was a potential marketing disaster that Canadian food scientists wanted to avoid altogether in the Americas. As a result, the name Canola was invented to describe a new hybrid of rape, and even more important, the name was trademarked. Unlike any other cooking oil, Canola's name is licensed to companies that produce the oil, so they have to pay money to sell it under that name. Those Canadians are a savvy lot.

Everyone Needs a Sensitive Frond

Is a touch-me-not plant a fern?

The incredible touch-me-not, probably one of the most fascinating common plants in the world, is a member of the mimosa family and isn't related to ferns at all. The touch-me-not, better known in some places as the "sensitive" plant, instantaneously closes its leaves and takes on a wilted look when touched. The plant will do the same in rain and sometimes with changes in light. As with other mimosa varieties—from bushes to trees—its flowers are hairy-looking, almost like pink or purple puffballs.

What does a sensitive plant look like?

Cute Little Furry Things

Ever wonder how porcupines have sex or why Hugh Hefner chose a rabbit for his *Playboy* mascot? Or how about why raccoons have black eyes? Wonder no more. Herein lie the not-so-fuzzy answers to these and other sordid little questions.

When Life Hands You Lemmings . . .

My older brother Carl is an idiot. He believes the old myth that lemmings commit mass suicide. They don't, right?

No, they don't. Tell Carl he's fallen for a myth. Sure, it's a deeply ingrained one: the metaphor of lemmings following the crowd to their death is so good that it's even used by people who know better. The reality is that lemmings don't commit mass suicide. Not even the really depressed ones.

Not that many people would care if they did, though. They're nasty little volelike vegetarians that reproduce like rabbits, popping out as many as thirteen babies every three weeks. There are other breeds of lemmings, including one that lives in bogs in the eastern United States and Canada, but the most famous is the Norway lemming, which lives in the tundra and grasslands of Scandinavia. These are the ones that are allegedly suicidal. However, in reality, that's wishful thinking–they are actually homicidal.

In the warm spring when grass is plentiful, the lemming population rises at an alarmingly unsustainable rate. By summer, desperation kicks in as food supplies dwindle, and things turn ugly. Adults fight to the death for breeding territory; lemming moms raid the nests of their neighbors and kill their neighbors' young.

Still, all this carnage isn't enough, and the animals must disperse in search of food and living space. They don't formally migrate en masse, it just looks that way. "A booming population of near-sighted, physically clumsy rodents stumbling down Norway's numerous funnel-shaped gullies is what produced the massive migration look," says an article in *Canadian Geographic.* While a number of lemmings may accidentally fall over the edge of a narrow mountain path or get washed away while fording fjords and streams, they don't intentionally kill themselves. Actually, most of the lemmings that die along the way are eaten by predators taking advantage of the free protein that just happened to amble by.

Isn't it true that a Disney film crew made up the myth about lemmings committing suicide?

People who blame a popular Disney nature series for creating the myth have inadvertently added still another layer of myth to the myth. Granted, the Disney people did a lot to spread the story. Disney cameramen filming lemmings for *White Wilderness* (1958) were instructed to "throw them over the cliff by the bucketful if necessary" to create the spectacle of thousands of lemmings tossing themselves into the ocean to drown. However, the Disney producers didn't introduce the myth; they were merely trying to re-create something they'd heard about, and which they themselves believed to be true.

In reality, the lemming suicide myth existed long before Disney. Lemming suicide stories emerged centuries earlier in Scandinavia, where people had witnessed masses of the clumsy animals falling and drowning. Over time, these myths became even more bizarre. Swedish archbishop Olaus Magnus, in *The History of Northern Peoples*, written in 1555, speculated that the only explanation for sudden explosions in lemming populations was that they descend from the sky. This echoes an Inuit myth about the collared lemming, which they call *kilangmiutak* ("that which falls from the sky").

Too bad Disney didn't show that!

Prickly Heat

How do porcupines have sex?

Is "*Very* carefully" the answer you're looking for? It's actually not as carefully as you might expect, although we wouldn't recommend trying this at home. For starters, mating is a dangerous pastime for male porcupines. They are one of many species who fight for the rights to mate with the receptive female, who, in the case of the porcupine, is receptive only once a year. The stakes are high in porcupine love, and the female enjoys inciting the rivalries. She hangs out in a tree, urinating and loudly calling to all the boys fighting each other down below. When one man's left standing, the female crawls down the tree. The male urinates on the female to excite her, and the female curls her tail over her back to expose her quill-free genital region. The male porcupine's genitalia are located on his underside, too, so when they mate, there are no quilly parts for them to be watchful of during the whole messy business, which takes no longer than a minute or two.

I've never seen a porcupine in the wild. Where do they live?

If you're in America (North or South), start looking up. American porcupines–often referred to as New World porcupines, quill pigs, or hedgehogs–make their homes in trees. The Old World porcupines, found in parts of Southeast Asia, India, Africa, and parts of Europe, live in tunnels underground. Contrary to the nickname *hedgehog,* the American porcupine is not the same creature as the hedgehog, although they share some similarities. Hedgehogs are insect eaters, whereas porcupines are herbivores. Hedgehogs are smaller, and the coarse hairs or quills on their backs are not barbed or dangerous; touching the back of a hedgehog is often compared to handling a coarse hairbrush. Hedgehogs are native to England and Europe, parts of Asia, and Africa. Only the domesticated hedgehog–the African pygmy hedgehog–can be found in America and is usually kept as a pet.

Mirror, Mirror

What's the biggest rodent of all?

The South American capybara, which can reach lengths of up to four feet. They've been compared to a guinea pig, a small boar, and have been nicknamed "water pigs." We think they look more like a mutated rabbit, actually. Whatever the case, they're the favorite lunch for creatures like the local alligator, the jaguar, and the human. The beaver is the second largest rodent.

Which group of mammals has the most species? Primates?

No, rodents. About half of all mammal species are in the order Rodentia, which includes such familiar animals as lemmings, rats, mice, squirrels, chipmunks, moles, and beavers. Bats, another large group of mammals, come in second, with about 900 different species. Compare that with a measly 180 different species of primates. Rats and bats scoff at the lowly little primate numbers.

Not without a Green Card

Are gerbils really illegal to own in California?

They are. The government fears—and rightly so—that if gerbils
were allowed to be bought, sold, and owned within the state,
then surely some would get loose. Since California is primarily
an agricultural state, wild rodents—particularly those that
propagate quickly—are a direct threat to crops. Don't point a
finger solely at California, though. It's illegal to own a gerbil in
Hawaii, too.

California doesn't single out gerbils. Other animals that
aren't legally allowed to reside as pets in this state include
snapping turtles, alligators, the African lion, skunks, prairie
dogs, squirrels of all types, and the dormouse, to name just
a few.

Of Mice with Men

*It's not like they have wheels leading to nowhere in
the wild, so how do mice know to run on wheels
in cages?*

Mice have an instinctual need to run. Their metabolism is fast,
and they burn off energy almost as fast as they consume food.
Fortunately, too, mice are quick learners. Curiosity leads them
to the wheel to explore. Once on the wheel, it doesn't take long
for them to reach upward and roll a couple of times. They soon
learn that the wheel will move continuously, satisfying their
need for physical activity.

*Since ancient Egyptians believed that things buried
with the dead went on to accompany the deceased in
the afterlife, did they apply this to their beloved cats,
too?*

They did. Found in tombs of mummified cats were rats and
mice for the cats to hunt in the afterlife. But the Egyptians
didn't want it to be all work and no play for their feline idols.
They also left saucers of milk in the kitty tombs so they could
lap in leisure.

More Mousy Characters

What were the names of Mickey Mouse's nephews?
Mortie and Ferdie.

Mickey Mouse is the most popular cartoon rodent, hands down. But who's the second most popular cartoon mouse, Jeeves?
Just cartoon *mice,* or all rodents? We'd have to give Rocket J. Squirrel of *Rocky and Bullwinkle* the thumbs-up if we're talking about all animated rodents. However, the mouse category is a bit more difficult with so many to choose from. Our favorite is Itchy from *The Simpsons,* but probably Mighty Mouse or Tom from *Tom and Jerry* should place second. Here are a few others: Pinky and the Brain, Ignatz Mouse from *Krazy Kat,* Hanna Barbera's Pixie and Dixie, Speedy Gonzales, Fievel, and DangerMouse.

Mousy Dung

How can I tell if I have mice or rats in my house?
Basically, mouse poop is smaller. But don't take our word for it. The Centers for Disease Control (CDC) has a nice picture guide to rodent poop that you can download and use as you look at droppings around your house. The CDC graph shows that usually about 11 mouse droppings fall in a cluster within a square-inch area. Rat poop, however, only has about 5 or 6 in the same space.

> **Which famous movie star was once a professional rodent exterminator?** We've heard Warren Beatty.

Rodent Addendum

Who wrote the children's song "Three Blind Mice"?
The English once believed that rounds taught children to concentrate. It's in this context that most scholars believe "Three Blind Mice" was written. The first written mention of it appears in 1609 in a melody book titled *Deuteromelia; or, The Seconde part of Musicks melodie.* The editor of this

work–and, many believe, the song's author–was a teenager named Thomas Ravenscroft.

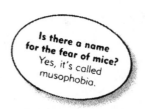

Is there a name for the fear of mice? Yes, it's called musophobia.

Gnawing Questions About Computers

Where does the Internet computer term Veronica *come from?*

It stands for Very Easy Rodent-Oriented Networkwide Index to Computerized Archives. The software was developed specifically to search gopher space. Gopher was the precursor to the World Wide Web and was named after the mascot of the University of Minnesota (the place it was developed). Veronica and another early search engine, Jughead, were used to search Gopher the same way that Ask Jeeves is used to search the WWW.

Why is the computer device called a mouse? Why not "handle," or even "egg," "slider," "pointer," or "button-activated input device"?

Because this great piece of technology was destined for cuteness, not boring drivel. Originally created in the late 1960s by Douglas Engelbart, it was dubbed the "XY Position Indicator for a Display System." Catchy, but early users quickly came up with a nickname of their own: "turtle." The animal motif continued with the more accurate description, "rodent," that followed. With its long hairless tail, the little pointer device resembled any number of creatures in the order Rodentia, and these early technogeeks didn't want to discriminate. However, good sense and a desire to sell to consumers took over, and the name was changed to "mouse," which stuck permanently. In every dictionary on our shelves we found *mouse*, which reads like this Merriam-Webster Dictionary on-line entry: "mouse: a small mobile manual device that controls movement of the cursor and selection of functions on a computer display."

Where can I see a picture of the legendary jackalope?

Splitting Hares

Why is the jackrabbit a rabbit and not a hare?

You are a very good student of the subtleties of the order Lagomorpha, indeed. Hares and rabbits are often wrongly identified, even by those in the know. For instance, the Belgian hare, a cute little domesticated animal that's been credited with starting the whole pet bunny craze in America, is actually a rabbit. And jackrabbits are not rabbits at all but hares. How can you tell the difference? A jackrabbit is born in a single nest aboveground. Its eyes are open, and fur already covers its body at birth. It can, amazingly, jump within minutes of being born, and begins to fend for itself at a rather young age. Jackrabbits are basically solitary animals and, like most hares, tend to have longer ears and larger bodies than true rabbits. Rabbits, on the other hand, are born bald, blind, and helpless within underground colonies. They are extremely reliant on their social infrastructure for most of their lives, and they tend to be smaller than most hares.

Where did Coney Island get its name?

In Old English, the word *coney* meant "rabbit." When the English came to the little island in New York, it was already heavily populated with bunnies, hence the name. There's yet another location that was named for rabbits: *spania.* This Carthaginian word gave us the name for Spain, which literally means "land of rabbits."

Why do magicians use rabbits in tricks instead of, say, guinea pigs or cats or mice or something?

We could say it was a tradition dating back to the druids, who believed rabbits had magical powers, but we'd be lying. Besides the fact that they're cute and docile, it's really because they don't make noise and therefore can't give away the trick.

Why are pet rabbits and guinea pigs prone to heatstroke?

Their cooling systems aren't as efficient as, say, a dog's or a human's. Dogs can pant to release heat and cool down their bodies. Humans release sweat from over 2 million sweat glands to keep their body temperatures regulated. Bunnies, however, don't sweat but rely on a system of rushing blood to their ears, where it's quickly cooled over the large, thin-skinned surface area and sent back to the rest of the body. Although this is for the most part effective, when temperatures rise and rabbits find themselves without shade, the process can't always keep up with their rising body temperatures. Guinea pigs also don't sweat, and their ears are quite small and inefficient for cooling their bodies. The only way to keep guinea pigs from suffering heatstroke is to make sure the temperature around them doesn't get above 90 degrees. They prefer it even cooler, with relatively low humidity while you're at it. Keeping a lot of fresh water and shade available for both rabbits and guinea pigs is a must.

Sketchy Past

Where did the Playboy bunny come from?

The magazine's original art director, Art Paul, drew the bunny for the second edition's cover. Hugh Hefner liked the furry rabbit because it looked frisky, playful, and had that whole multiply-like-rabbits thing going for it. Hefner was also instantly attached to it because the idea of a bunny in a tuxedo was different from other men's magazine mascots, none of which were animals. Art Paul later admitted that if he'd known at the time that the rabbit would become so synonymous with the *Playboy* empire, he might've spent more than half an hour drawing the cartoon.

> Where can I see the original *Playboy* bunny rabbit drawing?

I Put a Smell on You

What makes skunks smell so bad?

Six different compounds of sulfur and hydrogen make up the smelly skunk musk. The two musk glands, located near the skunk's anus, can squirt musk up to ten feet.

The odor especially permeates hair or fur (including wool clothing), because it reacts with animal protein, making it smell even worse. But that's just the beginning. Only three of the compounds stink at first spray—the other three have a delayed action that kicks in when they contact water, which makes washing counterproductive.

Is skunk spray dangerous?

Not to humans. However, to animals who depend on their sense of smell to hunt food, find and attract mates, or avoid predators, being sprayed makes them unable to pick up scents of any kind, leaving them vulnerable.

Like Rats in a Cajun

Do people in Louisiana really eat swamp rats?

Rural Louisianans have trapped and eaten the nutria—an orange-toothed rodent that inhabits Louisiana swampland—since its introduction to the bayous in the 1930s. Now the state government is encouraging nutria's role as the next exotic food out of the swamps by instigating a five-year program that pays trappers and processors by the pelt and pound to get rid of this swamp pest.

Nutria history in Louisiana goes back to 1937, when the founder of the Tabasco pepper sauce empire, L. E. McIlhenny, decided he'd like to get in on the nutria fur business that was sweeping Canada and Europe. He imported thirteen of the beaverlike rodents from Argentina and began a fur farm. The nutria, a quick-breeding rodent, soon numbered 150 at the McIlhenny place, and L. E. thought he'd struck gold. Unfortunately, a hurricane that struck in 1940 wreaked havoc with his dreams. The storm shattered the nutrias' cages, and they all escaped into the Louisiana swamp. McIlhenny was saddened, not only for himself but for the nutrias. He was convinced that the alligators would make a quick lunch of them.

How wrong he was. By 1960 nutrias numbered somewhere around the 20 million mark, and for two decades trappers harvested at least a million a year, which pretty much kept the population steady. After the 1980s fur market crash, however, nutria fur was never in demand again, and the rodent's numbers skyrocketed out of control. Today, it's estimated that there are at least 18 nutrias per acre of Louisiana bayou. Swamp vegetation, rice and sugarcane crops, bayou dams, and even sewer drainage systems are all being damaged by the large population of nutrias. There are so many they've become run-of-the-mill roadkill to most residents.

Because of this, the nutria's image is pretty badly squashed, which is the reason some view the government's program as a futile, money-wasting project. Proponents of the government plan, however, point to a couple of factors they believe make the nutria a dinnertime contender. One is that the French have been consuming nutrias for years. Their dish, *ragondin,* is a delicacy that some Americans are familiar with even if they are unaware of the main ingredient. Fine restaurants in Louisiana are now offering it on their menus without any double take from their customers, right next to leg of lamb and rabbit. Another encouraging historical note is that when both alligator and crawfish were introduced to the Louisiana public, they were almost laughed back into the swamp. Now, both are considered part of spicy delicious Louisiana cuisine.

But what does nutria taste like? Is it gamy? And how healthful could it be? Surprisingly, nutria has less fat and cholesterol than chicken or turkey and is loaded with protein. By all reports, it tastes like rabbit and is very tender. The last question, then: Which wine goes best with swamp rat? A good merlot is recommended.

| Where can I buy nutria meat? | |

But She Sure Is Fun to Dance With

Is it true nutrias have breasts on their backs?
The nutria's nipples are located rather high up on her front–almost to her back–so that her young babies can suckle without drowning, as she spends much of her time in water. The nutria is fast and agile in the water but rather clumsy on land.

A Cheeky Little Rodent

How many nuts can a chipmunk fit in its cheeks?

A chipmunk can fit up to 34 beechnuts, each about half an inch in length, in its cheeks at one time. Chipmunk cheeks are made of very elastic tissue, allowing the chipmunk to store a lot of food. When its cheeks reach capacity, the chipmunk will bury its stash somewhere and head back to collect more. This ensures that it will have enough food to sustain itself during the long winter months. In the spring, when the chipmunk comes out of hibernation, it finds the remaining stashes of nuts and seeds–if any are left–and consumes them. As you can imagine, the chipmunk often forgets where it buried everything, and new plants sprout and grow from these hiding places.

> Where can I find a
> live web cam that
> shows naked mole
> rats?

And the Eyes Have It

Why do raccoons have black eyes—or "raccoon eyes"—and why does my mascara always make me resemble this nocturnal species?

The fur around its eyes is black both for eye protection (the black is believed to keep out glare) and for camouflage, as it makes it difficult to see a raccoon at night, protecting it from predators. As for the mascara, try a brand that's water resistant, and try not to sweat.

Where does the name raccoon *come from?*

It comes from the Native American word *arakum*, which translates into "he scratches with his hands."

Barking up the Wrong Family Tree

Why is a prairie dog called a dog? Is it a member of the canine family?

The name comes from the doglike sound that the prairie dog makes, but the animal is actually a rodent. It's closely related to the squirrel, and the resemblance is striking. Although the ears are a bit smaller, and the tail is straight instead of bushy, these hole-digging herbivores are in essence ground squirrels. They are also on their way to becoming endangered in many of the states they inhabit. Why? Because of farming. Cattle farmers specifically worry that the prairie dog–which lives in large underground communities called "towns"–will consume their feed grasses. Also, farmers have tended to plow up their acres with little regard for the prairie dog towns that exist below the surface. And it has been common for the not-so-creative local yokels to use the prairie dog as target practice, carelessly endangering entire colonies. The prairie dog plays a major role in maintaining the ecological balance of the prairie. It's also the major food source for several prairie-dwelling species, like the bald eagle. For more information on this dying American species go to http://www.nwf.org/prairiedogs/dog_q&a.html.

Not Counting Politicians, Bankers, & Lawyers, That Is

What mammal has the smallest heart?

It would have to be one of the two smallest mammals on earth–either the bumblebee bat of Thailand or the Savi's pygmy shrew. Both are about the size of a bumblebee (or, to put it in better perspective, a large thumbnail) and weigh between 1.2 and 3 grams. The shrew is usually a bit smaller than the bat, which, when it spreads its wings, appears much larger than it is. Although their body parts, including their hearts, are small, these mammals have a larger heart-to-body-size ratio than any other mammal. What this means is that their hearts beat wildly–in the case of the shrew, an amazing 1,200 beats per minute–and their metabolisms are so fast that they have to eat constantly to avoid starvation. In comparison, the blue whale's heart rate is somewhere between 10 and 30 beats per minute, and a healthy human's resting heart rate is about 60 to 80 beats per minute.

What's a baby bat called? A pup.

Don't Bug Me, Man

People have long held up insects as beautiful and commendable things— while at the same time crushing, poisoning, swatting, and cursing them. Why bugs even waste their time on us after all that is hard to understand.

This Little Light of Mine

Are glowworms related to fireflies?

Yes. It's all in the family–quite literally. Glowworms are the larvae of fireflies (and, in some species, the flightless females).

The larvae take one or two years to develop before passing through a brief pupal state and becoming adults. As larvae, they eat earthworms, snails, and the larvae of other insects, killing their prey by injecting poison into them. After all that buildup, the adults (now fireflies) live for only five to thirty days. Adults eat nectar from flowers or, in some species, nothing at all. However, females of other species are cannibals (see below).

All 1,900 species of glowing insects are members of the family Lampyridae, which is a pretty good name for a bug that lights up the night.

Hey, There, Big Bug, Come Over after Dark for Dinner?

Why do fireflies glow?

Sex, mostly. Males fly around flashing the world in a pattern of dots and dashes that is very specific to their species. Female fireflies wait until a male flying nearby flashes the correct signal for their species, and in return, she flashes him with her own light. They meet and create beautiful luminescence together.

Well, most of the time that's how it works. However, the females of some firefly species prey on the males of other species. They lure the males by imitating the mating signals of the other species. A hapless suitor flying too close gets eaten.

Multiply by Dividing?

Is it true you can cut an earthworm in half and that both halves will grow back?

If worms could multiply by dividing, they could dispense with all that messy sex business. Worms are hermaphrodites, so they can mate with any other worm of their species, although not with themselves, as some believe. After mating, both will likely be pregnant, and they can each lay an egg capsule about a week later. After fourteen to twenty-one days, one to five baby worms will hatch out.

The reality is that the common myth is wrong. While some worms can regrow a tail if they lose it, the part that was lost dies. True, the lopped-off tail can wriggle around helplessly for a few hours, but that's just a dead worm walkin'—somewhat akin to a chicken running around with no head—and the tail will eventually stop moving. The other end with the head might also die from the injury, but at least it has a chance of surviving if its intestines and other vital organs are still intact.

Is there a name for a fear of worms? Helminthophobia.

Do earthworms see?

No. They have no eyes. However, they can sense light and dark.

Eaters' Digest Books

What did bookworms eat before there were books?

Think of what a difficult time it must have been for bookworms in the days of clay tablets and scrolls. We can imagine them sitting impatiently on empty shelves, waiting for centuries, and finally cheering in the fourth century A.D. when somebody got the bright idea of sewing sheets of parchment together, creating the direct ancestor of the modern book. . . .

Of course, bookworms don't eat just books, they also eat any number of other things, both natural and man-made. In fact, there isn't just one species called the bookworm; the term is used to describe a number of moth and beetle larvae that infest books and eat the glue and binding.

Makes us wonder, though, if computer bugs eat e-books, and if tapeworms eat audio books.

Anty-Pesto and Vermin-Celli

What's entomophagy?

It's the fancy name for bug eating. All of us do this accidentally all the time—check out the Food and Drug Administration's guidelines for acceptable levels of insect parts in common foods (e.g., a normal-size jar of peanut butter is legally allowed to contain up to 210 insect fragments before it's officially deemed unsanitary). However, more people than you might suspect eat bugs deliberately. And why not? Pound for pound, insects have more protein and less fat than beef.

Where can I see the Food and Drug Administration's guidelines about the number of insect parts allowed in food?

Besides tribal communities eating grubs, do people of any industrial nations actually eat bugs?

According to *Man Eating Bugs: The Art and Science of Eating Insects,* by Peter Menzel and Faith D'Aluisio, there are bug eaters everywhere. In Japan, they say, you can buy cans of baby bees and grasshoppers. In China, try the water beetles in ginger and soy sauce. Some Australians fancy sautéed grubs and naturally sweet honeypot ants. Thailand and Cambodia offer deep-fried tarantulas and water bugs; in Indonesia, salted dragonflies in coconut milk. And in the United States, you can get candied crickets.

He's an Art Larva

Who is the artist who tricks larvae into making cocoons out of gold and jewels?

Hubert Duprat. Since the early 1980s, he's been removing caddis fly larvae from their natural environment and providing them with precious materials instead of the twigs, sand, and dirt that they usually use when constructing their cocoons. The larvae create elaborate jeweled sacs, gluing them together with a sticky silk.

Where can I see artwork created by Hubert Duprat's larvae?

Oh, Goody, We Love Riddles

Here's a question I can't answer: I'm normally earthbound, but I have sex by flying straight up into the air. Only one in a million of us gets the chance to reproduce, yet we thrive nearly everywhere. Who am I?

You're a queen ant, of course.

Get Thee to a Buggery

I thought ants were supposed to be hardworking, but the ants in my ant farm are really lazy. How come?

They're not lazy as much as they are listless, depressed, and demoralized. If you want a human equivalent, imagine you're an employee at a failing business. You once worked with thousands of workers doing a variety of things, inspired by leadership that kept everything running smoothly. Suddenly, all of your friends have been laid off, the leader is gone, and you're part of a small skeleton crew that is barely completing rudimentary tasks. One by one, the workers around you are slowly dropping dead. How would you feel? Perhaps listless, depressed, and demoralized?

Ants are remarkably similar to office workers in this regard. A healthy queen exudes pheromones that keep an ant colony vitalized and happy. An anthill without a queen ends up sinking into apathy, and unless it can quickly replace the queen, the ants inside get conquered by another colony or slowly die out.

So if you want a healthy, happy, busy ant colony, you need a lot more space than your little plastic ant farm can offer. And you also need a queen.

If you want to see an ant farm done exceedingly well, visit the leaf-cutter colony at the National Zoo in Washington, D.C. Using multiple Plexiglas boxes and many yards of clear plastic pipes that go around and over visitors, the zoo has a thriving colony of about 4 million happy little ants.

> Where is the view of the ant farm at London's National History Museum?

Other zoos have similar displays. The National History Museum in London even has a live web cam with infrared cameras. Not surprisingly, you can see the ants best if you tune in during English daylight hours.

Ant We Got Fungus

What do leaf-cutter ants do with all those leaves?

If you've ever seen them at work, you do have to wonder: hundreds of thousands of ants chopping out pieces of leaves and relentlessly carrying them back to their colony. A nest of leaf-cutters, numbering up to 5 million strong, can completely defoliate a full-size tree in about a day.

The funny thing is that the ants don't eat the leaves. They can't digest them. Yet they bring no other food into their colony. What gives, you wonder?

Well, here's the deal with leaf-cutter ants: they're farmers. They use leaves as a medium upon which to grow the one food they do eat, the lepiotaceae fungus. The strange thing is that lepiotaceae doesn't grow anywhere else except in leaf-cutter colonies, because it has evolved to a point that it can't reproduce without the ants' help. The fungus helps convert the leaves into carbohydrates. In return, the ants keep the fungus alive by seeding shredded leaves with its spores. When a queen ant leaves to begin a new colony, she carries a supply of starter fungus in a special opening in her head.

For at least 23 million years, the ants and fungus have had this symbiotic relationship. It makes us look at both species in a whole new light.

A Monumental Weevil

Where is there a statue honoring the boll weevil?

Enterprise, Alabama. Because boll weevils destroyed the entire cotton crop in southern Alabama, local farmers were forced to try a variety of other crops that ended up paying better than cotton. In gratitude, they honored the little bug with a statue.

The monument, erected in 1919, reads, "In profound appreciation of the boll weevil and what it has done as the herald of prosperity."

The statue itself was originally a lady who looked a lot like the Statue of Liberty, standing thirteen and a half feet tall with arms upstretched. Finally, in 1949, local artist Luther Baker decided it would be a good idea to have an actual boll weevil be part of the Boll Weevil Monument. He took a bit of metal, made a giant boll weevil, and attached it to the lady's hands. It is, we're told, one of the strangest monuments you'll ever run across, and we ain't just whistling Dixie.

Equal Time for the Stinkbug!

Does Alabama really have a state insect? Is it the boll weevil?

It sounds like a joke, but most states do have official state insects. Some also have a state butterfly. Alabama's situation is particularly confusing: its state insect is the monarch butterfly, not the boll weevil, but its state butterfly is the eastern tiger swallowtail. Needless to say, most people who have been in the state would agree that the fire ant, mosquito, or chigger might have been the more appropriate choice.

But butterflies seem to be a trend among many states, as you can see below. Honeybees are popular, too, but nary a stinkbug, cockroach, horsefly, or mosquito among them.

Here are the others:

Alaska–four-spotted skimmer
Arkansas–honeybee
California–California dogface butterfly
Colorado–Colorado hairstreak butterfly
Connecticut–European praying mantis
Delaware–convergent ladybird beetle
Florida–zebra longwing butterfly
Georgia–honeybee
Georgia state butterfly–tiger swallowtail
Idaho–monarch butterfly

Illinois–monarch butterfly
Kansas–honeybee
Kentucky–viceroy butterfly
Louisiana–honeybee
Maine–honeybee
Maryland–Baltimore checkerspot butterfly
Massachusetts–ladybug
Mississippi–honeybee
Mississippi state butterfly–spicebush swallowtail
Missouri–honeybee
Nebraska–honeybee
New Hampshire–ladybug
New Hampshire state butterfly–Karner blue butterfly
New Jersey–honeybee
New Mexico–tarantula hawk wasp
New York–spotted ladybird beetle
North Carolina–honeybee
Ohio–ladybug
Oklahoma–honeybee
Oklahoma state butterfly–black swallowtail
Oregon–Oregon swallowtail butterfly
Pennsylvania–firefly
South Carolina–Carolina mantis
South Dakota–honeybee
Tennessee–ladybug and firefly
Tennessee state agricultural insect–honeybee
Tennessee state butterfly–zebra swallowtail
Texas–monarch butterfly
Utah–honeybee
Vermont–honeybee
Vermont state butterfly–monarch butterfly
Virginia–tiger swallowtail butterfly
Washington–green darner dragonfly
West Virginia–monarch butterfly
Wisconsin–honeybee
Wyoming–western swallowtail butterfly

My Kingdom for a Rotting Floorboard!

We hear about queen ants and queen bees, but not the king ant or the king bee. Do any insects have kings, too?

Ants and bees live in a matriarchal society where nearly every member–queen, worker, and soldier–is female. A few male boy-toys are allowed to live to service a new queen if necessary; but they aren't kings in any sense of the word. In the winter, when food gets scarce, the males are the first to be thrown out of the colony to die in the snow.

However, not all social insect colonies suffer from such a tyranny of female supremism. Ironically, the most fair, nonsexist insect society is that of the termites, who live up to our highest ideals, yet are poisoned, oppressed, and maligned by a world of humans intent on preserving its wood products. You see, termites have a gender-egalitarian society, with workers that are both male and female. Likewise, they have a king and a queen, bound together in a monogamous relationship seldom seen in the royalty of any species. Bee and ant queens mate just once, but very promiscuously–they take on all the guys they can find, then kill off the males during the mating process. With this, they manage to get enough sperm to last a lifetime. In contrast, the secretive termites have family values that would shame an upstanding Baptist preacher. The queen and her king mate for life, and they do it lustfully and regularly, keeping everyone happy and popping out an egg per second day after day.

Long Live the Queen

What insect can live the longest of all?

Termite queens. It depends on the species and the entomologist doing the estimating, but some say they can live fifty years, while other experts say seventy-five or even one hundred years.

We Can't Believe It's Not . . . Ooh, Yech!

Why the butter *in* butterfly?

Well, we can knock down one old story: it is *not* a spoonerism for "flutterby."

Butterfly comes from the Old English word *buterfleoge,* meaning "butter/flying creature." Some linguists speculate that maybe the *buter* refers to the butter-yellow color of some European butterflies. However, that doesn't make a lot of sense; plenty of colors besides yellow are represented in the butterflies of the Old World. The venerable *Oxford English Dictionary,* never one to shy away from a little scatology when the occasion calls for it, points out that the Old English name was a translation from a Dutch word *botervlieg* that was synonymous with *boterschijte,* "butter shit," speculating that the *butter* in the name came from the butterflies' oily yellow excrement, the result of a diet that consists largely of flower pollen.

> Where can I learn about the life cycle of a butterfly?

Better Bright Red than Right Dead

Why are butterflies so colorful? Doesn't that make it easier for predators to spot them?

You're right, it doesn't seem to make sense for anything so vulnerable to be so brightly colored. Why aren't they more like the other bugs, which blend so much into the background that they're nearly invisible to their enemies? Butterflies are so bright, it's almost as if they're trying to be seen.

It turns out, though, that high visibility can be a pretty good survival strategy—as long as you combine it with chemical warfare. Many butterflies are somewhat poisonous, but they're not necessarily poisonous enough to kill birds and other predators, just make them good and sick. So what happens is that a young bird may eat one monarch butterfly in its life, but after becoming violently ill it's unlikely to want to eat any more. The monarch's distinctive coloring helps make it memorable, so birds will easily associate the experience of getting sick with the monarch's markings. The butterfly that died in teaching the bird to never eat another monarch will not have died in vain, but in the service of saving scores of its peers from being eaten by the same bird. In fact, some birds will remember the experience so vividly that they'll vomit simply in response to *seeing* a monarch.

On top of it all, the martyred monarch also ends up saving members of another species from the same fate. The viceroy butterfly very closely resembles the monarch. It isn't poisonous, but its similarity to the monarch protects it from predators, regardless.

Where can I learn about the life cycle of a butterfly?

Ask

Etymology and Entomology

Why were body lice called cooties?

Leave it to American ingenuity to create a popular toy in the 1950s in which kids put together brightly colored plastic parts to create a comic replica of a pubic louse. The slang term came from English soldiers in World War I, who picked up the term from British sailors, who themselves picked up both the infestation and the native word for lice, *kutu,* while on leave in the Polynesian islands.

We suspect that *seam squirrels*–another slang term for the little creatures–also was coined by military men.

What is a dumbledore?

The headmaster at Harry Potter's school shares his name with an early term for the common bumblebee. *Dumbledore, bumblebee,* and *humblebee* were all onomatopoeic attempts to re-create the bee's buzzing sound.

Your Alligatorlike Children Will Burn

Why are they called ladybugs even when they're male?

It does seem like another one of those examples of insect sexism, doesn't it? And its alternative names in English are equally feminine: *ladybirds, lady beetles,* and even (for some reason) *lady clocks.* However, merely crying sexism isn't that simple.

During the Middle Ages, the insect-killing beetles were regarded as benevolent instruments sent by the deities. Several languages link the cute little red bugs with heavenly beings. For instance, the French call them *les bêtes du bon Dieu* ("creatures of the good God") and *les vaches de la Vierge* ("cows of the Virgin"). The Germans call them *Marienkäfer,* or "Mary's beetles." English people, similarly, called them "Our Lady's beetle," which became shortened with time to "lady beetles" and then "ladybugs."

Why did farmers have such a high regard for the ladybug? Credit their appetite for garden pests, especially aphids and scale bugs. An adult female can consume up to 75 aphids a day, while the smaller male may consume up to 40. Even the larva, resembling a tiny alligator, uses its large jaws for the good of the farmer: it chomps as many as 350 aphids before becoming a full-fledged bug.

Why Motorcyclists Are Gnatty Dressers

Why do little bugs congregate in clouds?

Gnats hang out in clouds in part to practice the safety-in-numbers self-defense ploy. Predators often get confused by having so many to choose from; furthermore, the gnats' victims (i.e., you and me) are less likely to do harm to any given individual gnat if dozens are biting them at once. Another reason is the same reason teens tend to hang out together: The world is a big place when you're a tiny fly, and if you're grouped together in a small clump, you're more likely to be able to find a willing partner when it's time to couple up. Gnat and teen courtship behaviors are similar in other ways; for example, male gnats will show off their desirability for mating by hotdogging and showboating, zooming quickly up to the top of the swarm and back down again.

The various species of gnats include biting midges, punkies, and no-see-ums, many of which can bite people quite painfully.

What is the song "La Cucaracha" about, anyway?

The song, beloved equally by children and the sandwich trucks that serve lunch to office workers, is about a pothead cockroach's wasted life, death, and funeral. Here are the words, as well as a translated version:

> *La cucaracha, la cucaracha*
> *Ya no puede caminar*
> *Porque no tiene, porque le falta*
> *Marijuana que fumar.*

> *Ya la murio la cucaracha*
> *Ya la lleven a enterrar*
> *Entre cuatro zopilotes*
> *Y un raton de sacristan.*

> There's a cockroach, there's a cockroach–
> His travel plans became a joke
> 'Cause he didn't have, he was missing
> Marijuana he could smoke.

> Oh, it killed the poor old cockroach–
> Brought him to the funeral house
> He was carried by four buzzards
> And the churchyard sexton's mouse.

Quick, Henry, the Deet

How many insects are there for every person on Earth?

One estimate pegs the number at about 10,000 bugs for every human being, which is no surprise to anyone who goes outside on a hot summer night. Over 1.5 million known insect species populate the world today, but entomologists believe there may be millions more out there waiting to be discovered and classified.

How many mosquito bites would it take to completely drain your blood?

If you're an average adult, about 1,120,000.

Little Bug Makes Big Noise

What do seventeen-year cicadas do during the 16.9 years that they're not outside making that ungodly racket?

Oh, you know—reading, doing the laundry, hanging around with friends, surfing the Net, partying. You'd be surprised at how quickly seventeen years can go by.

Seriously, the seventeen-year cicadas essentially do the same as the thirteen-year cicadas: they live as larvae a few inches underground, sucking nutrition from the undersides of tree roots.

What's strange is that entomologists haven't figured out the bigger questions about the cicada. For example, we don't really know why some of them are timed to an exceptionally odd seventeen-year cycle, while other, virtually identical, cicadas operate on an equally strange thirteen-year cycle. And we don't know how a huge mass of cicadas manage to emerge at exactly the same time thirteen or seventeen years after they went underground.

Of course, this strategy of emerging en masse works pretty well for them. As many as 1.5 million cicadas per acre can suddenly appear, overwhelming the ability of their natural predators to eat them. A myriad of spiders, snakes, birds, rodents, and other animals can eat their fill without putting any appreciable dent in the population (a phenomenon called *predator satiation* by the scientists who study such things). Then, after courting and mating, and each female laying up to 600 eggs in tree branches, the cicadas die off as quickly as they appeared.

Antlike nymphs hatch from the eggs and drop from the tree branches. They burrow into the ground until they find a tree root. After sucking its sap for the next thirteen or seventeen years, they heed some mysterious signal from inside or outside themselves, shed their exoskeletons, and emerge from the ground as cicadas. Amazing mysteries still abound.

How and why do cicadas make that damnable noise?

Yes, it is loud–loud enough to damage human ears, loud enough to drown out lawn mowers. But think how loud it would be if the female cicadas joined in. As it is, only the males make noise, and the silent females seek them out.

Cicadas make noise by stroking ridged membranes on the sides of their abdomens called tymbals. Their abdomens are hollow, adding resonance. Gathering in huge "choruses" (yes, this is the scientific term), usually on sunny tree branches, these bands of musicians quickly attract bevies of females who are ready to mate. Think of them as the boy bands of the insect world.

A cicada's hearing organs, by the way, are called tympana and are located on the bottom of its abdomen. You'd think they'd be deafened by all that racket.

Next Book, We'll Tell You How to Use a Toad as an Egg Timer

How do you use a cricket as a thermometer?

Well, first of all, don't stick it under your tongue–or anywhere else, actually. It will not give you the information you seek and nearly always damages the insect.

First some background. Cricket metabolism slows at a consistent rate when they get cold and speeds up when they get hot. This is true not just of crickets but all cold-blooded creatures. Crickets, however, make especially good thermometers because they do a predictable, repetitious thing–the lovesick males chirp regularly and incessantly. The intervals between chirps become an indicator of temperature–on cold nights the intervals increase; on hot nights, they decrease.

Here's how you can make this fact work for you. If you count the number of chirps from a cricket and do some simple math, you can get a moderately accurate sense of the temperature. Here's the simplified formula first, the one taught in nature class: to get a close approximation of Fahrenheit, count the number of chirps in fifteen seconds and add 40. If you prefer your crickets on a metric scale, count the number of chirps in a minute, add 50, and divide by 9.

But what if a good estimate isn't enough, and you want to make your cricket thermometer a precision instrument? Well, then, you have to calibrate it. First of all, determine what kind of cricket you're using. All of the results below give you the temperature in Fahrenheit:

- If your cricket is black, it's a common field cricket. Count its chirps for fifteen seconds and add 38.
- If it's small, pale green, and you found it on a tree, it's a tree cricket. Count the number of chirps in seven seconds and add 46.
- If it's white and it's in a tree, you're in luck—you've got a snowy tree cricket. This is considered the most accurate cricket of all. Count its chirps for fourteen seconds and add 42.

Just one final warning—the cricket thermometer is accurate only in summer weather, not in the chill of autumn. If there's snow on the ground and you hear zero chirps out there, you'd be foolish to do the math and conclude that the temperature is 40 degrees.

Hitting It on the Fly

You've claimed that insects have yellow blood, but when I squish a fly, I often see red liquid. What's that?
It's the pigment from your victim's eyes.

Gotta Fly

How fast can a fly fly?
You might as well ask, "How quickly can a flea flee?" When you're trying to catch a housefly, it may seem like it can take off at supersonic speed. Really, though, you could easily outrun one, or even outwalk it. Although its wings can flap 200 times a second, the housefly flies through the air at a speed of only about four and a half miles per hour.

What is the fastest insect?
The Australian dragonfly. How fast is it? It depends on who you ask. Experts estimate anywhere from a remarkable 35 mph to an unbelievable 60 mph.

Bee for the Pilgrims

Were there honeybees in North America before Columbus?
No. European settlers first brought honeybees to the American colonies in 1622. Over the coming years, many of the insects fled the regimentation of man-made hives and sought freedom in their own colonies throughout the New World. By the late 1700s honeybees had settled along most of the eastern half of North America. In the 1800s they fulfilled their manifest destiny by spreading their colonies from coast to coast.

How much honey does a bee make in its lifetime?
One to two ounces, or roughly a tablespoonful.

Pike's Pique

Does "Flight of the Bumblebee" come from a symphony or opera or something?
The maddeningly frenetic piece comes from an opera called *The Tale of Tsar Saltan* by Nikolai Rimsky-Korsakov. In the opera, the melody is played by a solo violin (not a trumpet, accordion, or piano, as in more popularized versions). Although the melody probably sounded like a bumblebee to whoever gave the piece its nickname, the opera contains no insects whatsoever. Instead, the "Bumblebee" piece accompanies a fight to the death between a man and a fish. Here's where it fits into the opera:

Tsar Saltan, who pretty much has a cameo role in his own opera, falls in love with the youngest of three sisters and marries her. He goes off to war and all but disappears from the plot for two hours. While he's gone, his queen's jealous sisters seal her and her young son in a barrel, which they throw into the sea. After floating for a long time, the barrel washes ashore on an island, and the queen and prince escape certain death. Time passes. One day the shipwrecked young prince, now a teenager, sees a beautiful swan being pursued by a large snub-nosed fish called a pike. While the violin plays its frenetic "Bumblebee" solo, the young prince fights the fish and saves the swan. She, of course, happens to be an enchanted princess,

How many crops in the United States depend on honeybees to fertilize them? More than fifty.

presumably on the lam from a production of *Swan Lake* down the street. The swan gives the prince magical powers, enabling him to build his own "Wonder City" on the island, complete with citizens who (not surprisingly) select him as their leader. The young prince convinces the swan princess to share his throne, and they live happily ever after, etc. Meanwhile, Tsar Saltan finally returns from war, hears about the fabulous Wonder City Island, and journeys there to be reunited with his queen and son just in time for curtain calls. Bravo!

Take This Thread Seriously

How long is the thread from a single silkworm cocoon?
If carefully unraveled, a single thread can average about half a mile in length. The poor little silkworm does all that work and ends up giving its life so someone can have a polka-dotted necktie. The general rule of thumb is that 10 pounds of mulberry leaves can feed 200 worms that will spin a pound of cocoons that will make about 100 miles of the very thin thread.

A Terrible Finish Indeed

Where does the red dye called cochineal come from?
It's made from crushing red-colored scale beetles that live in and on the prickly pear cactus.

How many shellac beetles do you have to crush to make a pound of shellac?
About 150,000.

Under the Sea

On this earth, there's a virtually unknown world we've just barely begun to explore, filled with strange creatures that aren't like us at all. No, we're not talking about Toledo, Ohio, we're talking about the world's oceans—an exotic foreign land that covers more than two-thirds of our globe.

Nuclear Fishin'

My uncle caught a fish, and it exploded like a balloon. What was that about?

Ah, the joys of deep-sea fishing—sun, surf . . . and exploding fish.

It's true. Some deep-sea fish will explode when you pull them out of the water, and no, it's not a practical joke played by Neptune's teenage sons. Here's why it happens: most fish keep their equilibrium in the water with an air bladder that balances their body mass and makes them essentially weightless, neither sinking nor floating to the surface. This is energy-efficient for them in that they don't have to continuously flap their fins and tails to stay at a desired depth.

Deep-ocean fish need a lot of gases in their bladders to withstand the increased water pressure that pushes on them from all sides in deep water. While they are able to make subtle adjustments to the amount of air inside their bladders, they can't do it quickly enough when they're caught on a hook and dragged suddenly toward the surface. As their bodies pass underwater from significant pressure to a middling amount of pressure, their bladders expand more and more, sometimes killing them before they even reach the surface. Finally, water pressure is removed completely when the fish is pulled out of the water. Blam! Fish parts everywhere.

Not all deep-sea creatures explode, mind you, because some don't have bladders. Sharks don't have them, for example, so they have to

Where can I see the video of the famous exploding whale?

continuously move if they don't want to sink to the bottom of the ocean. Skates and stingrays also don't have air bladders, but that suits them fine–they flatten themselves to the ocean floor when resting and then "fly" through the water by actively flapping the fish equivalent of bird wings. So if you catch a shark or a stingray, or if you decide to stick with those fish that live near the water's surface, you don't have to come home from your fishing trip covered with fish guts. And believe us, that'll please everyone–the fish, your fellow passengers, and you.

A Trout . . . No Doubt?

How closely are trout and salmon related?

Pretty close. In fact, so close that fishermen and scientists alike have trouble classifying the individual species. For example, take steelhead and rainbow "trout." They are actually the same fish–the name *steelhead* is used if the fish is able to make it to the ocean, and *rainbow* refers to those that are landlocked away from saltwater. In 1989, when DNA tests showed that the rainbow/steelhead isn't really a trout after all, the fish was reclassified as a salmon. Likewise, the Atlantic salmon was determined not to be a salmon after all, but a trout. Finally (as if you need another example), the sockeye salmon is called the *kokanee* or *silver trout* when it resides in fresh waterways.

Was salmonella so named because you can get it from salmon?

No. It got its name from Dr. Daniel Elmer Salmon, an American veterinarian who isolated one type of the bacteria in 1885.

How do salmon get over obstacles when swimming upstream?

As you probably know, salmon make their trek to lay their eggs. Spawning before dying is a pretty good motivator, and salmon are pretty strong fish. The fact that they can leap up to twelve feet out of the water helps them overcome most obstacles. However, dams without fish ladders damn them to frustration and then extinction. Even without dams, life's hard for the poor salmon: when fingerlings–fish younger than a year old–are released from hatcheries, only about 1 to 5 percent make it back home to spawn.

Up and Away, Junior Bird Fish

Do flying fish really fly, or do they merely glide?

Flying fish are rather amazing creatures, capable of bursting out of the water and soaring hundreds of yards over the waves at a speed of about 35 mph. They do this when they've been startled by faster natural enemies such as tuna, bonito, and marlin and want to escape immediate danger in the water (although they also increase their chances of being picked off by seabirds). But are they really flying?

Technically, most of the 50 species of flying fish glide, although they do have a cool trick that can keep them airborne indefinitely–they swoop down, slip only their tails into the water, and with a swift flick, propel themselves up and away again.

Okay, that's *most* flying fish. But not all. Slow-motion film has revealed that a few exceptional species truly do fly, including the South American hatchet fish and the freshwater African butterfly fish. Both flutter their winglike fins to stay aloft. True, since they can't actually breathe out of the water, you don't see them flying in formation over the skies of Wichita, Kansas, but they do fly nonetheless.

Go Deep—Really Deep

How deep can fish live in the ocean?

So far, the deepest anyone's found a fish has been 35,800 feet below sea level, or about 6.78 miles down. Because the water pressure is stupendous, people haven't explored much under that level, so we don't yet consider this the definitive answer.

Herring Aid

How did some irrelevant fact come to be known as a red herring?

Red herrings are not a specific type of fish, but refer to any herring that's been smoked. The meat turns red and gives off a pungent odor, sending any but the truest lover of the dish running for fresh air. Hunters learned that dogs could easily follow the scent of smoked herring for long distances, and so the fish was often used as a device for training hounds.

It wasn't long before another group got wise and also began using this smelly fish to their advantage. Runaway criminals would toss red herrings away from their paths to throw tracking dogs off their scent. "Red herring" came to be known as a diversionary device of any sort, whether tactical or conversational.

Maybe We Should Keep Willy Locked Up after All

At animal shows, how do they train killer whales to jump onto dry land?

You'd think it would be hard. Animal trainers observe natural behaviors and reward those they seek to get the animal to perform again on cue. But when in nature would killer whales encounter a situation where they would deliberately beach themselves and still survive? After all, whales that beach themselves in nature usually do it accidentally–disoriented, scientists believe, by sickness, water turbulence, or even fluctuations in the earth's magnetic waves from sunspots. Whales that are beached in the wild usually end up dying, since they are often unable to free themselves, so any natural proclivity toward self-beaching shouldn't survive within the species for long.

However, there are exceptions to that general rule, and the killer whale is one of them. To begin with, killer whales aren't really whales. It turns out that they're a kind of dolphin, so people who are hip to what's shaking in the marine world now call them *orcas.* This is an important distinction in that as nonwhales, they don't have to swim around sucking up huge quantities of krill, but can go looking for red meat instead. And so they do.

These cute black-and-white dolphins ruthlessly live up to their "killer" name. They'll attack whales much bigger than themselves, for example, grabbing them by the mouth and ripping out their lips and tongues. They'll ram ice floes with great force to dislodge seals, penguins, and in at least one case, dogs, hoping they'll fall into the water and thus into their deadly grasp. There are even reports of orcas turning traitor, helping human whalers trap whales in exchange for a cut of the meat. Them orcas is no good, we tells ya.

Believe it or not, this is all relevant to answering your question. In their relentless quest for fresh meat, orcas *do* sometimes beach themselves naturally. It's one of their favorite maneuvers at seal breeding grounds. Imagine the confusion at the local seal beach when a giant killer whale suddenly leaps out of the water and belly-flops into their midst with a great thrashing and gnashing of teeth. After chomping down on a few cute little seal babies, the orca can use its powerful fins to slide back into the dark waters.

This is the natural behavior that animal trainers reinforce. You may want to keep this in mind the next time you attend a water show and someone asks for a volunteer to hold up a fish.

Natural-Born Krillers

What does a crab-eater seal eat?
Despite its name, the crab-eater eats krill.

What exactly is krill?
It's ironic that whales, the world's biggest mammals, can exist
on some of ocean's smallest creatures. Krill are various small
shrimp that live in great swarms, which can be bigger than
Manhattan. There are about ninety species of krill, ranging
from three-eighths of an inch to six inches in length.

Call Me Dr. Ishmael, D.D.S.

How can you tell how old a whale is?
The most accurate way is to extract
one of its teeth and cut it in half,
since most marine mammals
grow a new layer of tooth each
year. As with a cross-section of a
tree, you can count the rings and
know how many years the whale has been
swimming the seas. Unfortunately, since whales seem to have
an aversion to dentistry, the hardest part is figuring out how to
keep them in the dentist chair.

How long do whole teeth grow? Usually three to ten inches.

You Gotta Have Heart

Which animal has the biggest heart?
The blue whale. Its heart is about the size of a VW Beetle. It's
surprising you don't see them doing more charity work.

What Sits on an 800-Pound Gorilla?

*Throughout all time, what was the biggest animal to have
ever dwelled on Earth?*
As far as we know, the modern-day blue whale is the all-time
champ, bigger than any known dinosaur or Ice Age creature.

To put things in perspective, the blue whale can grow to the length of a cargo jet (about 100 feet long) and the weight of three of them (150 tons). Its tongue is so big that about four dozen people could stand on it. But despite its monstrous size, the blue whale is not monstrous. As a matter of fact, it doesn't even have teeth. Instead, it has large keratin plates called baleen on its upper jaw that filter out krill. The whale swallows gulps of ocean water (up to 50 tons of water at a time) then spits it all back out, but the krill stay behind in the whale's baleen. Doing this over and over, it can eat up to 8,000 pounds of krill per day–about 40 million of the little creatures. So, to the krill at least, perhaps the blue whale is monstrous after all.

If it's so nutritious, why don't people eat krill?
Force of dietary habit, and because the fisheries of the world haven't yet figured out a cost-effective way of catching it. It's probably better this way, though, because we have no idea what effect our consumption would have on the ocean-dwelling species that depend on krill for survival.

Charles, Bring Us More of Those Yummy Whale Eggs

If beluga whales are mammals, then how do people get caviar from them?
Good question. Beluga whales are mammals, and like all but two species of mammals, they don't lay eggs. So you're right, it would be impossible to slice them open as we do fish and pull out their eggs to salt, pickle, and sell to status seekers with too much money. But the word *belukha* means "white" in Russian, meaning there are more things named beluga than just the whales, including the beluga sturgeon, from which beluga caviar comes.

Besides caviar, there's another thing that the upper classes deem beluga sturgeons worthy of dying for: when their air bladder is massaged and beaten just right, they produce a superior quality of gelatin called isinglass.

Picky, Picky, Picky

What's the difference between a dolphin and a porpoise?
Not much. Porpoises are slightly smaller. Also, dolphins have a
sharp snout and cone-shaped teeth, while porpoises have a
rounded snout and spade-shaped teeth. The differences are so
subtle that it almost makes us wonder if the people in charge of
delineating species don't have a little too much time on their
hands.

*How is a seal different from a
sea lion?*
Seals have shorter, fatter
flippers and no visible ear
flaps, and are often smaller
than their cousin the sea lion. See editorial note in answer
above.

Where can I see a
photo gallery of
different types of
fish?

Eight-Legged Race

Are squid a kind of octopus?
No, but they're both mollusks and cephalopods (meaning they
have eight legs). Squid have a hard inner-body shell called a
pen, instead of an outer one like clams and snails. The octopus,
in contrast, has no shell at all. Its outer mantle, or skin, is thick
and tough, protecting its boneless, fleshy body.

*If I were going to a cephalopod race, should I bet my
money on a squid or an octopus?*
Squid. Octopi are smooth, gliding along on their tentacles like
an eight-legged Fred Astaire, but they're no match for the
squid. Squid can shoot water backward like a rocket engine,
pushing them forward in great bursts of speed. They can travel
through the water at about 35 mph (about as fast as a bicycle
going full speed down a hill), and can even leap up out of the
water if so inclined.

Which is bigger, the biggest octopus or the biggest squid?
The giant squid, nearly sixty feet long, is bigger than any
octopus. Of course, both come in a variety of sizes. On the
small end of the size continuum, the pygmy octopus is the
Chihuahua of the cephalopod world, measuring only five inches

wide with arms outstretched. It likes to find an empty
clamshell and hide inside, closing it using the suction of its
suckers.

I have a bet with my optometrist—which animal has the biggest eyes?

The giant squid. Their eyes are the size of an extra-large pizza,
hold the anchovies.

Forewarned Is Forearmed . . . Times Two

Does an octopus's ink serve any purpose other than darkening the water for camouflage?

Standard procedure is for the octopus to simultaneously squirt
the ink, change skin color as camouflage, and jet away. As good
a job as the ink does of hiding something as hard to hide as an
octopus, it's also poisonous to some creatures and stuns others,
even when diluted in the vastness of the ocean. How poisonous
is the ink? If released by an octopus caged in an aquarium, the
ink would kill everything inside the glass walls . . . including
the octopus itself.

How else does an octopus defend itself from other animals?

If a good inky defense isn't enough, an octopus can go on the
offensive with its tentacles and a beaklike mouth. Although it
has no teeth, an octopus can take a chunk out of you when it
bites, and some have poisonous saliva that can immobilize or
even kill larger animals. In a battle between a shark and an
octopus of the same size, bet on the octopus. It'll win almost
every time.

How often have people been attacked by octopuses?

You mean like in the movies, where the giant tentacles wrap
around a person and pull him/her down into the octopus's
garden? Except for the always treacherous rubberized
special-effects kind, there's no verified record of an octopus
actually doing this.

Ironically, it isn't the giant octopus you need to watch out for,
but a tiny one that's small enough to fit inside a lunchbox
thermos bottle. Found in the South Pacific, the blue-ringed

octopus is petite, colorful, and cute enough that people sometimes decide to pick it up and get a closer look. It isn't until they get bitten and find themselves severely dead that they discover the blue-ringed octopus is perhaps the most poisonous of all.

Octopi Takes It on the Puss

I was taught as a child that more than one octopus are octopi. *Now, though, it seems that* octopuses *has become widespread. (In fact, the notorious Microsoft Word spell check marks* octopi *as incorrect.) Is this all part of the dumbing down of America?*

Not in this case. *Octopi* for *octopuses* always sounded funny to the ear (the singular sounded plural and the plural sounded singular). Even those of us who knew the rule tended to avoid using *octopi* because it made us sound like pedantic brainiacs.

So it is both satisfying and deeply disquieting to learn that our English teachers were wrong: *octopi* wasn't really correct after all. *Octopus* is based on the Greek words for "eight" and "foot." Substituting *-pus* with *-pi* may be something you'd do in Rome, but when in Athens, do as the Greeks do. In Greek, the plural of *octopus* should be *octopodes*. However, not even scientists, linguists, or brainiacs say "octopodes," so the next best thing (considering the language we're speaking) is using the English construction for plurals: *octopuses*. Although *octopi* is still sometimes used, it seems to be on its way out.

It Must Be Jelly 'Cause Jam Don't Shake Like That

What is the most dangerous jellyfish?

While most jellyfish can cause illness and skin damage to people, run-ins with the box jellyfish, found in Australia and Southeast Asia, are likely to result in death. There are three reasons for this. First, it is nearly transparent and difficult to see until it's too late. Second, its venom is more poisonous than that of other jellyfish. Finally, it has as many as 60 tentacles that are unusually long–up to ten feet. These tentacles instinctively wrap around anything that stumbles too close and immediately start pumping out venom. The result is that thousands of millions of stingers kick in to deliver poison through all parts of the victim's body at once. Youch.

Why is it called the Portuguese man-of-war?

In the 16th, 17th, and 18th centuries Portugal was a world naval power, and the man-of-war was a class of large, elaborate fighting ship. A typical man-of-war had four or five masts, high decks, and two or more tiers of guns. The sea creature came to be known as the Portuguese man-of-war because sailors at the time noticed a resemblance between the animal and the sailing ship. It even has a crest on top that looks like a sail (in fact, it *is* a sail, used by the animal to passively let the wind carry it along, which is a reason it can be found in tropical areas all over the world).

However, just as the Portuguese man-of-war is not at all a ship nor Portuguese, it's not even a jellyfish. In fact, it is not even really a creature: each man-of-war is actually a collectivist commune of individual, independent cells working together for the good of all.

Here's how the colony begins: a single larva hatches from an egg. Any larva *could* become one of several types of cells, but the first larva always grows into a blue gas-filled balloon. Floating in the ocean, carried along by the tropical winds, the single organism starts budding off clones of itself. These clone creatures hang from their floating older sibling, and each takes over a function that helps the whole. Some turn into tentacles for stinging and catching fish; others into tube-shaped "stomachs" that digest food and distribute nutrients according to need; others produce egg and sperm to spread the man-of-war's glorious revolutionary socialism to another generation. There's no other animal-like organism quite like it.

Which is more poisonous, a cobra or a Portuguese man-of-war?

The Portuguese man-of-war's venom is only about 75 percent as strong as the cobra's. Although the sting is rarely fatal, it can cause extreme pain, severe skin rash, nausea, and breathing difficulties. However, here's a weird thing: the man-of-war stays dangerous even when washed up on the beach. That's because its modular nature (see above) allows some parts to stay alive, active, and ornery, even though other parts might be dead or dying. So unlike a dead cobra, a "dead" man-of-war can strike out and sting you silly.

Shark Treatment

Are sharks mammals like whales and dolphins?

It seems like they should be, doesn't it? But no, they're fish.

Which shark is the most dangerous to humans?

Going solely by reported shark attacks on people, the great white shark is the most dangerous, followed by the bull shark, tiger shark, great nurse shark, and lemon shark. To be fair, though, humans kill millions of sharks for every human killed or injured by sharks. Consider human folly as well: the nurse shark, number four on the list of dangerous sharks, is normally a peaceful soul that lies on the bottom of the ocean and eats crustaceans. According to the *World Book Encyclopedia*, "Nurse sharks . . . have attacked people. But most of these attacks were caused by the victim, who foolishly grabbed a motionless nurse shark by the tail."

How did nurse sharks get their name?

Oh, we had high hopes for this one, we really did. Something along the lines of "their markings look a lot like nurse uniforms of the 18th century," or "they've been seen nursing small marine mammals back to health," or even "their oil was often used by mothers as milk for their children, making them the first (really wet) wet nurses." But such an answer was not to be. This is what we found: In medieval times, any shark or dogfish was generally called an *hurse* (with a silent *h*) because archers prized their oily skin for when they wanted to *hurse* ("smooth and polish") arrows. Over time, *an hurse* became "a nurse," and the term slowly became applied to the one species as people developed other uses and other names for the individual species.

Why don't scientists ever find any ancient fossilized shark bone?

It's not because there weren't sharks way back when. It's because sharks don't have bones. Their body is supported by cartilage only, which doesn't fossilize. Scientists have found ancient shark teeth, however, indicating that many of the shark species living today are quite similar to species that lived during the Cretaceous period more than 100 million years ago.

Vitamin A, Delivered C.O.D.

Cod-liver oil showed up in a lot of old movies and books as something parents often gave to their unwilling kids. How come it isn't used anymore?

Both shark oil and cod-liver oil were very commonly used as supplements for vitamins A and D. However, scientists in the 1940s figured out how to cheaply manufacture the vitamins, thus saving generations of kids from having to choke and gag on spoons full of the fishy, slimy liquid.

Salt and Battery

How much electricity could you get from an electric eel?

Oh, about 350 to 650 watts. But before you start looking for a place to attach an electrical outlet, you would need a surge protector first: an electric eel typically delivers only three to five bursts of electricity when it discharges, each lasting only about one-five-hundredth of a second. So that makes it useless for almost everything we can think of. Well, maybe it could be used as a stun gun–its voltage is enough to temporarily stupefy a human being. However, doing so would be a waste of wattage for the eel, since it mostly eats frogs and small fish.

By the way, the electric eel isn't really an eel at all, but a fish related to the carp and catfish. It is also not that unique–scientists have identified about 500 other species of fish that can also generate electricity.

One Thing or an Otter

If sea otters don't have blubber, how do they keep warm in cold water?

It's the same thing that almost drove them to extinction: their thick, luxurious fur. The otter has an unbelievable density of fur, with an estimated 650,000 hairs per square inch of its body (a human's scalp has a mere 1,000 per square inch). Natural oils in the dense fur repel water and trap tiny air bubbles, providing insulation. And to think we thought it was just vanity that keeps an otter carefully grooming its fur for nearly half the daylight hours.

The otter used to be far more prevalent than it is today. The animal was once found up and down the Pacific coast until hunters and furriers reduced its total worldwide population to about 2,000 in the early 20th century. Since then, government protection kicked in, and the otter population is now up to about 150,000.

Because it relies so much on its fur, the sea otter is one of the hardest-hit animals after an oil spill. The oil mats down its coat, destroying its insulating properties and making the otter prone to death by hypothermia.

Shellfish Pleasures

Can crabs swim?

A pitiful few members of the blue crab family have paddle-shaped legs that allow them to row through the water. The huge majority of crabs, however, cannot swim. They sink firmly to the bottom and walk across the ocean floor.

Why do lobsters turn red when they're cooked? Is that the color of their blood?

Actually, lobster blood is colorless unless exposed to oxygen, when it develops a bluish tint. Lobsters are mostly gray, green, or brown when alive, but never red. Boiling them breaks down the pigments that color their shells. The most durable heat-resistant tints are the carotin-based reds, so they're the last to disappear during boiling. This is also true for most other hard-shelled crustaceans like shrimp, crab, and crawfish.

Do lobsters have to be boiled alive to make them safe to eat?

No. Unrefrigerated lobster meat turns bad faster than other types of edible flesh, which is why the cruel tradition of boiling them alive began centuries ago, before the advent of refrigeration. Nowadays they can be killed humanely without going bad before boiling. In fact, currently most lobsters are killed and frozen right on the boat without a discernible change in flavor or texture. But, even then, beheading them at or immediately following their death does keep them fresh longer.

How long does it take for a lobster to grow to full size?

Lobsters are a little different from you and me (this is assuming, of course, that neither of us is a crustacean). They start out looking like tiny bugs, smaller than crickets; they grow and molt along the way. That is, they get too big for their shells and shed them periodically, like snakes shed their skins. While they are in between shells, they grow quickly by absorbing a lot of water.

The lobsters shed their shells twenty-five to thirty times in the first five to seven years of their lives, gaining about 15 percent in length and 40 percent in weight each time. At the end of that time, they weigh about a pound, and the interval between molts gradually lengthens to about once a year. This process goes on for the rest of their lives. A hundred-year-old lobster can be three feet long or longer.

There's a lot of shell in the way. How do lobsters mate?

It's during the soft-shell phase after shedding that females mate. The courtship process is sweet. When she is ready to molt, the female approaches a male's den and stands outside, releasing her scent in a stream of urine. When he emerges from his den, the two spar briefly, then the female places her claws on his head to let him know she is ready to molt and mate. They enter his bachelor pad, and she languidly strips off her shell. He tenderly turns her limp, yielding body over onto her back with his legs and his mouth. The male, still hard-shelled and passionate, passes his sperm into her body with a pair of rigid and grooved *swimmerets*–small appendages normally used for swimming. Afterward, she sinks into the soft warmth of the ocean bed and stays in the safety of his den for about a week. When her new shell is hard again, she calls a cab and goes home.

The sperm she received from the male goes into a special repository, where it stays viable for two years. When she decides that conditions are right to settle down and have a family, she fertilizes her eggs, numbering from 3,000 to 100,000. She carries them first in her body, then (for another nine to twelve months) under the swimmerets attached to her tail until they hatch. Her larvae float for a month after hatching, then settle to the bottom to turn into lobsters proper. Still, their odds are not good—for every 100,000 eggs hatched, 4 to 6 typically survive long enough to get up to a one-pound weight.

Is it true that lobsters mate for life?
Lobster romances end the minute the female walks out of her mate's den of love.

Lung Time, No Sea

I know a whale is a mammal, but where are its nostrils?
A whale's nostrils are what we call its blowhole—therefore, on top of its head.

How long can a sea turtle stay underwater without coming to the surface for air?
If swimming, a few minutes. If resting, as long as two hours.

Not counting amphibious animals, what water creature can live for the longest time out of water?
The longest known case is about 10,000 years, a record set by some brine shrimp. Brine shrimp, also known as "sea monkeys" in toy stores, can go into a form of suspended animation if caught outside the saltwater where they make their home. Some desiccated brine shrimp, determined to be 10,000 years old, were found by oil drillers near the Great Salt Lake in Utah. Although there was no measurable sign of life, the little sea monkeys came back to life when placed in saltwater. They were, of course, dazzled by all the technological progress that had taken place in Salt Lake City during the intervening time.

Koalas & Kangaroos, Wombats & Wallabies

Hopping for the Best

Why do kangaroos hop instead of run?

One reason kangaroos don't run is because they can't, even if they wanted to. Their legs have evolved to a point where they're completely unsuited for doing so. Luckily, when the lush

Australian rain forests dried up and became desert, kangaroos were particularly well suited to the terrain. Kangaroos needed to be able to travel great distances to find the quantities of food they required, to support their large bodies, and it turns out that hopping requires about 25 percent less energy than an animal of similar size uses when running. To add to its energy efficiency, a kangaroo's digestive organs bounce backward and forward with each hop. How does this help? Well, the back-and-forth lurching mechanically pumps its lungs, saving the energy that kangaroos normally have to expend for breathing in and out.

How far can kangaroos hop?

Up to thirty-three feet per jump, for a maximum speed of about 40 mph.

These New Parents Are *Really* Jumpy

How big is a kangaroo baby when it's born?

Not so big. It's larger than a lima bean, but smaller than a full-size peanut. And it's not

> Where can I see photos showing the development of a baby kangaroo?

cute at all, unless you're the kind of person who finds slimy pink intestinal worms irresistibly adorable.

Kangaroos are marsupials, as are most of the mammals that are native to Australia. Besides looking pretty weird, how are marsupials different from the others? Most mammals are *placental,* meaning the fetus develops in the womb and is fed directly from its mother's bloodstream by a placenta. Hundreds of millions of years ago, though, marsupials went down a different evolutionary path. Instead of giving birth to well-developed young after a long gestation period, marsupials give birth to tiny, hairless, helpless, blind, nearly larval young after a much shorter gestation. Looking like undeveloped fetuses, the young are instinctively capable of only two things after being born: crawling up the fur of their mom to the safety of her *marsupium* (pouch), and finding a nipple there to suck upon.

In the case of a kangaroo, gestation is only thirty to forty days, and then the little joey attaches itself to the mother's teat for six or seven months. After that time, the baby finally grows into a miniature version of its parents. It begins leaving Mom's pouch for short hops before returning for food, rest, and safety.

Other marsupials have similar developmental patterns involving short gestation, a long time in the pocket, then gradual integration into the world.

Double Your Pleasure, Double Your Fun

I read that male marsupials have forked penises. So how do they . . . well, you know?

Male marsupials do have forked penises. The other strange thing is that their testicles generally lie in front of their penises instead of in back like other mammals. So how do they have sex? Well, it turns out that there's somebody for everybody, and marsupials are no exception: female marsupials have two uteri and two vaginas that share a common, fork-shaped opening. The birth canal forms from an opening in the connective tissue between the two vaginas.

Planet Marsupial

Do all marsupials have pouches for babies?

All marsupials have pouches, but not all pouches are equal. For a marsupial like the kangaroo, which spends most of its time standing upright on two legs, the marsupium opens toward their heads like our shirt pockets, so that gravity helps keep the baby in. However, for four-legged marsupials that dig in the ground, the pouch faces away from their heads, which makes their babies' climb from the womb easier and keeps dirt out.

Are any marsupials native to Europe, Asia, or Africa?

Nope. Of the 260 known marsupial species, just a couple live in the Americas, and the rest live in Australia and the Australasian islands that surround it.

If the vast majority of marsupials live in Australia, how did a few of them get to America? Swim?

The only native North American marsupial is the opossum; the only other marsupial that doesn't live in Australasia is the shrew opossum of South America. All others live in Australia and the surrounding islands. The two American marsupials, however, didn't swim from Australia.

Most scientists believe that marsupials first appeared in the Americas and then traveled to Australia. This happened so long ago that Australia was still connected to a much larger land mass consisting of the Americas, Antarctica, and Australia. So the theory is that the forebears of the Australian marsupials spread to Australia via Antarctica. (Antarctica wasn't yet located at the South Pole, and the climate wasn't as chilly.)

The problem was that, for whatever reason, marsupials didn't compete very well when pitted head to head with the placental mammals. As a result, in the Americas, marsupials were all but wiped out. However, Australia didn't have many placental mammals, and the marsupials were able to thrive, evolve, and dominate.

The last great battle between the placentals and the marsupials is currently taking place in Australia, and it threatens once again to turn into a rout of the marsupials. In the time since placental mammals like rabbits, sheep, cows, wolves, wild dogs, and humans were imported to the continent, native marsupials have steadily been losing out on their home turf, and many are considered endangered.

Wallabies & Wannabes

Are wallabies and wallaroos the same as kangaroos, or are they like kangaroo wannabes?

They're all members of one big happy family (Macropodidae, or "big foot"). There are about fifty-five different species of kangaroos and near-kangaroos. The differences among them are not particularly apparent–they're pretty much determined by their size and where they live:

- Kangaroos are generally bigger–up to 185 pounds for the red kangaroo–and they prefer congregating in large groups on open, dry, grassland plains.

- Wallaroos are more stocky and not quite as tall, and they live in small groups in hilly country.
- Wallabies are much smaller—some as small as rabbits—which works out pretty well since they hang out in places without much traveling space, like dense forests and thick vegetation along rivers and lakes. They also live in small groups.

Be warned, though, that even these distinctions have exceptions—for example, since the tree kangaroo lives in the forest and is smaller than most other kangaroos, it should arguably be called a tree wallaby. Sometimes the people who make up names for things just don't play by the rules.

Does the tree kangaroo really live in trees?

Once, before the Australia forests turned into deserts, all of the kangaroos lived in trees. Scientists believe that eventually they all hopped down, and that at some point in history the tree kangaroo reverted backward in the family's general evolution, climbing back into the trees, where it now spends most of its time.

Is the kangaroo rat a native of Australia?

No, it's a North American rodent. A tad confusing, no doubt. However, the rat kangaroo is an Australian native. Kangaroo rats live in the deserts of the southwestern United States and Mexico. Rat kangaroos live in the swamps and deserts of northeastern Australia.

Was Captain Kangaroo supposed to be Australian?

We guess that you're asking because of his name, but sheesh—Captain Kangaroo Australian? Can you imagine the once-popular TV host turning to Mr. Green Jeans and saying, "Mate, why don't you and Missus Green Jeans come by, and we'll put Bunny Rabbit on the barbie"? We think not. In the 1950s and '60s, *Captain Kangaroo* paved the way for quality kid shows like *Mr. Rogers* and *Sesame Street.* Host Bob Keeshan was a Long Island native, and his character was supposed to be a retired American sea captain. He was called Kangaroo because his coat had big marsupial-like pockets from which he'd pull various props (carrots for Bunny Rabbit, for example).

Neither a Burrower nor a Wombat Be

What kind of a bat is a wombat?

The very worst kind of bat, in that it is not a bat at all. A wombat is the common name for three different species of burrowing Australian marsupials, the largest of which can grow up to three feet in length. They superficially resemble what you'd get if you crossed a guinea pig with a stocky little dog.

Wombats are both loved and hated by the humans who coexist with them. They're loved because they tend to be docile and easily domesticated, so some people keep them as pets; however, they're hated by farmers, who believe that the little burrowers do damage to their crops. Although it's true that wombats deserve a share of the blame for eating some crops, it's likely that rabbits are doing the bulk of the damage. Regardless, as a result of competition with rabbits, the efforts of farmers, and damage done by cars, in some areas of Australia the wombat has been all but eradicated. Wild wombats are now considered an endangered species.

The Devil You Say

Are Tasmanian devils as ruthless as they seem to be in Bugs Bunny cartoons?

If you can't trust cartoons, what can you trust? Taking into account cartoony exaggeration, Tasmanian devils are about as aggressive as portrayed on the screen. They have sharp teeth, strong mouths, and a bad attitude, and they kill their prey by clamping down on the back of the head and crushing the skull. Besides hunting wallabies and possums, the Tasmanian devil will also eat any carrion it runs across, bones and all.

The strange thing is that the devils are as aggressive to each other as they are to their prey. This is true from the moment of birth. As marsupials, they're born just a little bigger in size than a grain of rice. That's not necessarily a problem, since they only have three inches to travel from their mother's birth canal to her pouch and nipple. The bad news is that as many as fifty babies are born at a time, and there are only four teats available. The brothers and sisters jostle each other in a mortal race–the first four clamp inseparably onto the nipples, and the rest die of starvation.

After six months, those lucky and aggressive four become independent of their mothers, but then they have new worries. A high proportion of these young marsupials get attacked and killed by adults of their own species. Tasmanian devils have pink ears that turn bright red when they're angry and powerful jaws that can crush bones, allowing them to devour whole animal carcasses–meat, fur, bone, and all. That is, if another Tasmanian devil doesn't kill it first. Mortal combat over carcasses is not at all uncommon.

Makes the cartoon Taz look warm and fuzzy by comparison.

What's interesting is how well Warner Brothers voice man Mel Blanc managed to get the sound of a Tasmanian devil right–a cross between Scooby Doo and an accelerating Harley. Search for Tasmanian devil sound files on-line, and you'll see what we mean.

> **Where can I hear Tasmanian devils and other Australian animals?**

A Platypus by Any Other Name

Does any mammal lay eggs?

There are sometimes discomforting exceptions to general rules. For example, virtually all mammals give birth to their young. However, take careful note of the "virtually" in the last sentence–of the 4,500 known species of mammals, 4,498 of them deliver their babies live. The two that don't are related to each other, and both are Australian, but one is famous while the other lingers in relative obscurity.

The famous one is the duck-billed platypus, which has caught fickle public attention largely because its name sounds like a punch line waiting to happen. (Other animals like the yellow-bellied sapsucker and the blue-footed booby have gained similar celebrity.) Granted, the platypus has other idiosyncrasies to keep people amused. For example, it has the bill of a duck (actually, just an extra-hard bit of hypersensitive skin), no teeth, flipper feet, and a flat beaverlike tail. Mama platypus doesn't have nipples; she merely leaks milk sloppily through patches of skin, and the baby platypuses lick the milk from her wet fur.

The platypus is odd, and its cousin the echidna is equally strange. It also lays eggs and has no teeth. Unlike the platypus, though, the echidna has quills like a porcupine and a sticky tongue that laps tongue and the roof of its mouth. But despite these curiosities, the echidna is still fairly unknown. Perhaps it would help its public relations efforts if the echidna went by its alternative name, the spiny anteater.

> **What are platypus eggs like?**
> Sort of leathery, like snake and turtle eggs.

What does the platypus use its bill for?

The rubbery bill makes it possible to shovel up mollusks and other edibles from the muddy depths. It has been discovered recently that the platypus's bill has thousands of touch-sensitive and electrosensitive pores. The latter can detect weak electric currents from the muscle activity of prey and perhaps even electric fields from water flowing over stationary objects. This is a good thing because—yet another funny thing about the platypus—it closes both its eyes and its ears when it hunts underwater.

What did the first settlers think when they first saw a platypus?

We don't know what the aborigines thought when they first saw what they called a *tambreet* (or *boonaburra* in the Mallangong language), although an aboriginal myth about how the platypus evolved has to do with a teenage duck disobeying her father by going ashore and getting raped by a water rat.

We know that when British settlers saw the platypus near the Hawkesbury River in 1797, it ignited controversy for nearly a century. The Brits first called it a watermole and speculated that it was somehow a cross between a reptile, fish, bird, and mammal. The Australian governor had some killed and preserved and sent them to England for zoological study. The outraged scholars believed they were being hoaxed. One suggested that the specimens were a "freak imposture" sold by Chinese taxidermists to gullible travelers. Another took a pair of scissors and, believing that it was merely glued on, tried to pry the "duck's bill" off the corpse of one. (The marks of his efforts can be seen on the specimen, which is still on display at the British Museum of Natural History.) After five years of debate, the scientists grudgingly conceded that maybe the animal wasn't really a fraud and gave it the common name

Where can I see dancing cartoon platypuses?

platypus, which is Greek for "flat foot," and the scientific name *Ornithorhynchus anatinus (ornithorhynchus* is Latin for "bird-billed").

Still, it took another eighty-two years before a Scottish zoologist actually went to Australia and confirmed that the animal laid eggs and fed its newly hatched babies milk. His conclusions were controversial–after all, the animal's lack of nipples would seem to make lactation impossible–but both were eventually proven true.

And a Lot of Lonely Shepherds

When I went to New Zealand, there were an awful lot of sheep. How many are there in proportion to the number of people?

There are more than 13 sheep for each of the 3,853,116 people who live in New Zealand.

Prepare to Be Emused

Is the emu the mascot for Eastern Michigan University?

Alas, there are no Fightin' Emus at EMU (nor are they the mascot of the other significant EMU, Eastern Mennonite University). That's too bad, because the name would sort of make sense, and not just because of the EMU initials. After all, Eastern Michigan University in Ypsilanti is overshadowed by its larger, more prestigious relative–the University of Michigan in nearby Ann Arbor–in the same way the emu, the world's second-tallest bird, lingers in obscurity under the shadow of its taller cousin, the ostrich.

But "the EMU Emus" was not to be. Instead, the school's teams have been saddled with an achingly unoriginal bird name: the Eastern Michigan University Eagles. Of course, it could be worse. The other EMU calls its teams the Eastern Mennonite University Royals and uses a lion as its logo. Makes you wonder what they're teaching in colleges nowadays.

Free as a Bird!

If I wanted to set my parakeet Alfred free in his native habitat, would I take him to Africa or South America?

Australia. And don't call them parakeets, mate—it tees off the Australians. Their real name is *budgerigar,* or "budgie" for short. Although they've been bred in captivity into a bird of many colors, most wild budgies are green.

No, and It Doesn't Require a Chinese Goose, Either

My uncle says the fruit is called kiwi because it has to go through a kiwi bird's digestive system to sprout. Is that right?

Your uncle is either pulling your leg, misinformed, or thinking of the dodo tree. The kiwi fruit isn't even a native of New Zealand, as the bird is. The fruit really comes from southeastern China. It was called the Chinese gooseberry until it was transplanted to tropical places around the world in the early 1900s. A grower in New Zealand noticed that it resembled the shaggy, round kiwi bird. He started calling it kiwi fruit, and the name stuck.

Meet Me in the Eucalyptus

Is the koala bear more closely related to the grizzly, the polar, or the brown bear?

None of the above, or all of the above, depending on how you want to look at it. Although cute and teddybearlike, koalas are no more related to bears than they are to elephants. Koalas are marsupials, and their closest living relative is the wombat.

What do koalas eat?

Eucalyptus leaves and shoots. But they're fussy, eating only a few of the 500 species of eucalyptus in Australia. They obtain liquid from eucalyptus leaves and rarely drink water. In fact, the word *koala* comes from an Australian Aborigine word meaning "doesn't drink."

Do kookaburras really eat gumdrops, and what's a gum tree?

Oh, you've been singing old camp songs again, have you?

First of all, *gum tree* is another name for the eucalyptus that is so beloved by koalas. *Gumdrops* are the fragrant seedpods. However, kookaburras don't really eat them except in the lyrics of songs–instead they mostly eat large insects, mice, birds, snakes, and occasionally fish. At least the song has the laughing part about right–the kookaburra's common nickname is "laughing jackass," and with its braying it is considered a noisy pest in the quiet residential neighborhoods of Australia. You've probably heard the bird on television and movie sound tracks–its raucous laugh often shows up as a sound effect in jungle scenes set in Africa or South America, thousands of miles away from its native land. "Laugh, kookaburra, laugh, kookaburra, gay your life must be!"

Why Missionaries from the Snake Handler Cult Never Return from Australia

How many of Australia's 140 species of native snakes are poisonous?

Most of them. Of the world's top twenty-five most poisonous snakes, twenty-one of them are in Australia, including sea snakes that are two to ten times more poisonous than cobras. A hazard of the Australian beach, they compete with sharks, cone shells, ozone-depleted carcinogenic sunshine, and deadly jellyfish to be the first to send tourists to an early grave.

A Dingo Ate My Baby!

What was the first non-native species imported to Australia by people?

It was the dingo, and as with subsequent importations, the results have been somewhat disastrous to the native animal populations. What makes the case of the dingo more interesting is that it was brought to Australia as long as 50,000 years ago by aborigines who emigrated from Asia and brought their dogs with them. Some of the dogs escaped and went feral, becoming what are now called dingoes. The dingo eventually displaced a native marsupial carnivore called the Tasmanian wolf, driving it to extinction and taking over its spot in the food chain.

Do dingoes really eat babies?

Wild dogs the size of English setters, dingoes hunt wallabies, sheep, rabbits, and anything else they can catch and drag away. In 1998 a dingo was accused of dragging a baby a few feet toward the bush before being chased away by the infant's parents. In a celebrated murder case in 1980, the parents claimed that it was really a dingo that killed their baby. In real life, the parents were first convicted of the murder and then cleared on appeal, but whether a dingo was really involved has never been formally resolved. So the short answer is that dingoes probably *could* drag away a baby and eat parts of it, but it has not been proven that they ever *have*.

Crash!

Is there really an animal called a bandicoot, or was it invented by the PlayStation company?

Yes, Virginia, there is a bandicoot. It's another of those Australasian marsupials. Twenty-one different species go by that name, including the pig-footed bandicoot, the rabbit bandicoot, which is endangered, and the Ceram Island long-nosed bandicoot, which is thought to be extinct. Too bad *real* bandicoots don't come with multiple lives and a replay button.

Beasts OF Burden

So what do you know about the pack llama, the mule, or the water buffalo? Even though they work alongside people, we really don't know as much as we should about these animals. For instance, what happens when you cross a pony and a zebra? How did the reindeer get its name? Don't know? Read on.

A Camel Walks into a Bar . . .

Why do camels have humps?

Despite what you might've heard, camels don't really store water in their humps. Instead, the humps are big chunks of fat. Sure, it looks funny, but it's a system that works. In the desert camels may have to go for days and weeks without food, so the humps act as a storehouse of energy.

Why isn't a camel's fat distributed all over its body, as with almost all other animals? Ask any polar bear, and he'll tell you that fat also makes a really good insulating jacket. That's why polar animals tend to look more like sumo wrestlers than ballerinas. As you can imagine, the last thing a camel wants in the desert is a layer of warm fat all over, so it's evolved to a point where it's localized its fat into one (if Arabian) or two (if Asian) high-cholesterol lumps on top of its back.

Other unusual heat-coping features keep camels the preferred ship of the desert. For starters, their kidneys are designed to absorb an unusual amount of moisture in their urea. Also, their body temperature rises from 95° F at night to more than 104° F during the heat of the day–not an unusual thing with fish and amphibians, but almost never seen in mammals. Only at the higher temperature do camels begin to sweat, and when they do sweat, they lose moisture evenly from all tissues of their bodies, instead of just from the blood like most mammals. This allows a camel to lose 40 percent of its body weight in water before its life is endangered. It makes up this loss with binge drinking, staggering into an oasis and sucking down as much as fifty gallons at a time.

Does the hump start to disappear if a camel doesn't have any food and water for a long time?

It doesn't disappear completely, but it gets floppy and bounces around from side to side.

Spitting Image

Why do camels' eyes look so soft and sweet?

The camel eye is well adapted for its desert existence. It has a double set of eyelashes to keep the sand out and an inner eyelid that blinks to wash away any stray grains. Its eyebrow protrudes over the eyeball, shading it from the glaring sun. All of these things combined give the camel eye a large, gentle look that makes its cutesy-wootsy wittle face iwwesistable.

Do camels really spit?

Camels are very territorial, and if they feel threatened, they do spit, mostly at each other over food, but sometimes at humans if angry or hurt. Fair warning: if you do get caught in the crossfire, it can be pretty smelly, as camel spit consists of bile from its stomach mixed with saliva. Contrary to popular myth, camel spit will not burn or blind you; it's pretty harmless. But consider yourself lucky if the camel stops at spitting. An angry camel can be fairly dangerous, biting, kicking, and trampling. If one does spit, it's its way of saying, "Get out of my way, or I'll really hurt." Best to heed the spit and split.

Why do camels always twitch their noses?

It's not because they're sniffing the air or because they're bored. They're actually conserving water, believe it or not. When the camel exhales, it can close its nose and reabsorb some of the moisture from its outgoing breath before blowing out the carbon dioxide.

Do camels chew their cud like cows? They seem to always be chewing something.

Camels do ruminate–or chew their cud–but they are, confusingly enough, not considered true ruminants. They have only three separate stomach chambers, which, in part, keeps them from being classified with other ruminants, which have four chambers. The stomachs, though, function in a similar way, receiving unchewed food as filler and, after letting it sit in their stomachs for a while, burping it back up to be chewed and redigested. It's like two meals for the price of one.

Sailing, Sailing, over the Bounding Dunes

Why is the camel called the "ship of the desert"?

There's the obvious reason: camels can make it across a desert carrying goods, as a ship crosses an ocean. That said, if you've ever ridden a camel, you will see another very clear similarity between a camel ride and a ship voyage. Camels move the legs on each side of their bodies together–their two right legs step forward, and then their two left legs follow. This is different from many other four-legged animals, which move diagonally opposite leg pairs together. As a result, the camel's motion is extremely rocky. Many travelers have tales of "seasickness" upon their first few rides aboard the hump of the desert ship.

What do the Bedouins call the camel?

Ata Allah ("God's gift"). The Bedouins have over 160 distinct words in their language to describe camels and their traits.

This Doesn't Look Like the Hay We Got Yesterday . . .

Were camels and donkeys really at the manger when Jesus was born?

We can't speak for the donkeys (who can, really?), but their presence would've been likely. After all, it was a hotel stable, and we can assume there were all sorts of manger-using animals hanging around and wondering what the heck was taking place in their food dish. Even if the hotel guests weren't traveling with donkeys, remember, at least one ass would have been present—the one Mary rode in on. The camels' presence, however, is iffy. Romans and Jews didn't use camels much. The wise men from the East who are said to have come to see the Christ child didn't get there until much later. If they had arrived on time, the novelty of the situation would've attracted more people—not only to see the baby, but to gawk at the kings and their camels. As a result, the story would've been much bigger, than it was at the time.

The day Jesus was born wasn't even recorded until a hundred years or so after his birth, so the two gospel writers who included the story in their narratives weren't able to confer with any eyewitnesses. Christmas was not celebrated by Christians until well after the story was written down, placing the holiday that many more years after the actual incident. And even after Christ's birth was honored, the nativity scene, filled with all the players—Mary, Joseph, the shepherds, the wise men, the sheep, donkeys, and camels—didn't become part of that tradition until more than a thousand years later. Saint Francis of Assisi can be credited with adding the nativity scene to the celebration in 1223.

Were camels ever used in the United States for anything besides exhibits at zoos?

Yes, they have a long history in this country. Many natural history experts believe camels actually originated in North

America 40 million years ago and migrated north and west through Alaska and into Asia along with many other large animals prior to the Ice Age. More recently, though, camels were used as pack animals in the deserts of the western United States. In 1855 then secretary of war Jefferson Davis appealed to Congress for money to purchase camels so the army could build a wagon trail from Texas to Colorado. Congress consented and gave the army $30,000 for the purchase and transport of seventy-seven camels to Texas from the Middle East, along with a native fellow named Hadji Ali to help lead the camel caravans. Sadly, the Americans didn't try very hard to correctly pronounce his name, and he ended up being forever remembered in the history books as Hi Jolly. (In fact, you can see his pyramid-shaped grave with the name Hi Jolly if you pull off the interstate in Quartzsite, Arizona. Or go to http://www.findagrave.com/pictures/3063.html).

How did the camels do? The rocky American desert soil was different from the sand dunes the camels were accustomed to, and harder for them to navigate. Also, the camels sometimes spooked the American men and their donkeys. But despite these setbacks, the camels worked out pretty well. When the secretary of war requested funds from Congress in 1858 for 1,000 more camels, it looked like the camel might become a fixture of the American West. However, brewing tensions between the North and the South were monopolizing the government's attention. The funds were never appropriated, and the army camel experiment died a quiet death. Camels were used to map out a couple of specific western regions as late as 1860, but most of them were auctioned off or let loose in the desert, many to be shot by miners as pests.

Today there are small camel trekking companies that will take you on tours. One leads small caravans through the Big Bend expedition trail that was carved out by Lieutenant William Echols in the late 1850s with camels by his side. Tour guides narrate the history of the army camel experiment along the way while the camel below you adds its own commentary.

Gross Anatomy

How do veterinarians perform an operation on a camel if the camel can't lie flat on its back?

In the Dubai Camel Hospital at least, it's done on a slab with a hole in the center. The operating slab is tilted and turned so that it fits down over an upright camel. The hump goes through the hole in the center of the table. While the camel is knocked out, the table mechanically moves back around into a flat position, allowing the camel to do what it can't normally do in nature: lie on its back with all four legs in the air.

The camels at our zoo look like they're losing big chunks of hair all the time. Do camels get mange like dogs, or something?

Mange is a fairly common problem with camels, dogs, and a few other animals. It's caused by a skin mite that burrows into the skin and results in itching, loss of appetite, hair loss, and white sores. This condition is very difficult for the camel and can ultimately lead to death if untreated. The good news is that mange is easy to diagnose and treat, so you don't often see mangy camels in zoos. Our guess is that you visited the zoo in the spring or summer when the weather is warmer, and what you're seeing isn't mange at all but the normal shedding of the camels' winter coats. It can look alarming if you don't know what's happening: A whole chunk of hair can hang off the camel for quite some time, making it look as though the large beast is falling apart. Camels can lose as much as five *pounds* of hair in a season. Believe it or not, this wool is considered valuable as clothing fiber. What looks so grotesque when falling off the camel looks darn pretty when it's woven into a coat or a kicky beret.

Are camel hair paintbrushes made from camel hair?

Most cheap school-grade camel hair paintbrushes are made from a pony's tail or mane. Better-quality camel hair brushes include hair from an ox, pony, ferret, goat, and squirrel, or any mixture of these. But almost never a camel.

Cameltown Racetrack's Five Miles Long—in Dubai, Dubai

Are camels fast?

They can be. At the beginning of races, camels have been clocked upward of 40 mph. This pace slows considerably as the race progresses, however. The average speed of a racing camel is about 25 mph. A camel usually averages about 2 to 3 miles an hour when simply walking, 9 or 10 mph when trotting, and 16 mph during a gentle jog. A pack camel can cover about twenty-five miles per day, on average.

Who'd win the race, a horse or a camel?

Both the horse and the camel have been clocked at similar racing speeds: between 35 and 40 mph, with the fastest horse running just a little bit faster than the fastest camel. You're not the first to ask this question, by the way. In 1892 a horse and a camel competed in a famous one-day, 109.4-mile race in Australia. The horse won by a hair, then promptly collapsed and died. The camel, though second, crossed the finish line relatively unfazed by the experience. So the answer may be: In a 109.4-mile race, the horse will win, but in a 110-mile race, bet on the camel.

Wild Thing!

How many camels are there in the wild?

In their native habitat, it's estimated that there are only about 500 wild Asian camels and no Arabian ones at all. However, outside their native habitat, it's a different matter. Australians recently introduced the dromedary camel to the Australian desert, and there is a growing feral, or wild, population on that continent.

Will That Be One Hump or Two?

What would happen if you mated a one-hump camel with a two-hump camel?

You'd get a *nar*. They are often used as a transport animal in Central Asia. A nar is much like every other camel, but it has a single elongated hump.

Can you cross a llama with a camel?

Sure, but not easily. First, the basics: Camel sex is difficult, as these things go. The male can't ejaculate unless his penis is all the way into the she-camel's cervix, not just the vagina. The female has to be totally receptive to sex (a condition she finds herself in more often than the male, actually) for this to even be attempted by the male, and the intercourse has to be rigorous enough to jar her body into ovulating. After that, gestation is long–thirteen months–and it takes years before baby camels reach full maturity. It's no wonder then that camels, in general, are less interested in sex than other mammals that have a more rewarding time of it.

Trying to figure out a successful sexual experience between a camel and a llama makes the mind boggle. The size difference alone makes it nearly impossible to mate a large, aggressive dromedary with a small llama, or vice versa. However, a crackerjack team of camel fertility scientists have managed to do it despite the odds–just without the actual physical contact. Using artificial insemination, the first half-camel, half-llama was born in Dubai in January 1998. His name is Rama, since he was born under the full moon of the Ramadan holiday. The scientific name for such a beast? It's a *Camelus-Lama* hybrid, otherwise known as a *cama*. Oh, what a world we live in!

Llama Glama Ding Dong

What's the world's oldest beast of burden?

The people in the Andes mountains have been using llamas for at least 5,000 years, probably making them the first large domesticated pack animal, according to those who study these things. Other domesticated animals preceded the llama–sheep, pigs, dogs–but they weren't used to haul stuff like the llama was.

> What's the scientific name for a llama?
> Lama glama.

"The Dried Llama Meat Boys"

Where did the word jerky *come from?*

It comes from the Quechua (AmerIndian) word *charki*, meaning "dried llama meat."

Vicuña Mattata

What animal is on Peru's national coat of arms?

The coat of arms features three images that represent the three kingdoms of animal, vegetable, and mineral. A cornucopia of gold and silver coins is on the bottom; the native quina tree is at the top right; and the wild vicuña–a type of llama–is to the left. The coat of arms is also the centerpiece of the Peruvian national flag. Llamas can be found on the backs of some Peruvian coins, as well, particularly the one-sol coin.

Is a vicuña simply a variation of the llama?

It is, but it's smaller and more stocky. In South America it's used primarily for its wool. Since it's wild, many Peruvian towns hold annual capture-and-shear festivals where all the men go out and round up the wild llamas, bring them into city corrals, and shave them. Sounds like some frat parties we've heard about.

Of Llamas and Lliquids

How long can a llama go without water?

Unlike the camel, the llama has to drink water every day. It can go without food for a while, but the llama is a mountainous creature, not built for hot, arid places.

Never Spat with a Llama

How do you know if you're about to get spat on by a llama?

There are telltale signs, for sure. For one, ask yourself, "If I were a llama, would this behavior of mine scare me or make me so angry I could spit?" If the answer is yes, that's the first danger sign. The second is that the llama's ears will be laid back some, and its head will dart up as if stretching its neck. You'll soon hear a gurgling noise, which is the llama actually accumulating spit and bile from one of its stomach compartments. At this juncture, we recommend that you either duck and cover, or run fast. We assure you that once you've been spat on by a llama, you won't want to find yourself in the situation again anytime soon.

Alpaca Llama & Go!

Will it injure a llama to pack too much weight upon it?
Doubtful. Llamas have this great mechanism that kicks in when you load them with more weight than they can handle: They just sit down and refuse to budge.

How much does it cost to lease a llama?
Most places don't allow you to rent one of their animals without a guide and a specific trek in mind. The ones that do, require a class in which you learn about the care of llamas, or proof that you've had experience on treks with llamas in the past. Also, there are transportation costs to cover. If you can meet all of these requirements, expect to pay about $35 per day for llama, saddle, and packing gear.

> Where can I find llama treks in my area?

The Highest Llamas of All

What kind of llama lives in Tibet?
The only one we know of would be the Dalai Lama (one *L*), no relation to the animal llama (two *L*s), aside from the spiritual connection that comes from being brothers who dwell on this Earth. Tibet does have yaks, however, and people often mistake the two because they both have long fur (forgetting the fact that a yak's as big as an ox and has horns, mind you). Yaks are used for hauling, and for their milk, cheese, meat, hide, and fur.

The Greater Buffalo Area

Does the water buffalo ever spend time on dry land?
Water buffalo don't actually live in the water like hippopotamuses. However, they do enjoy wallowing in mud and shallow waters to cool down, which may be where they got their name. Unlike other buffalo, the various types of water buffalo are relatively docile creatures and easy to tame. Their large feet and short, stocky legs make them ideal for plowing in rice paddies and hauling things through muddy places.

Reindeer Games

Why are they called reindeer?

Because they belong to the deer family, and they can wear reins.

If reindeer are herbivores, how do they survive the hard, frozen winters?

They dig in the snow for lichen, a symbiotic alga-fungus growth that forms on the sides of rocks and trees. (The light green, paperlike moss you see growing on trees and rocks in the United States is one type of lichen, for instance.) This growth is the reindeer's main dietary source when snow covers the ground.

How many wild reindeer are left in the world?

None, but that's only by a technicality. Reindeer are by definition smaller, domesticated caribou, which means technically that there are no "wild" reindeer in the world. So what do people do with captive reindeer, you may be wondering? Think of them as an arctic camel. Their feet are wide and well suited for trudging through the snow and slush, making them the ideal pack animal for anyone who lives north of the treeline. Like camels and cattle in other parts of the world, they are also used for milk, hide, and meat.

Many northern nomadic tribes in Russia, Mongolia, and Scandinavia tailored their lives around the nomadic rhythms of the reindeer for thousands of years. Some still do. These extreme northern cultures are under threat of extinction, however, due to international land boundaries and modern technology. Although some tribal communities continue to do things the old way—from using parts of the reindeer for clothing, tools, shelter, and food to migrating with the roaming herds—it's also not uncommon today to see parka-clad tribe members on snowmobiles with radios.

Where did the name caribou *come from?*

It's believed to have come from its Micmac Indian name *xalibu*, "the one who paws," hinting at the caribou's trait of pawing in the snow for lichen.

When did "Rudolph the Red-nosed Reindeer" become part of the Christmas tradition?

Rudolph made his debut in 1939. Not surprisingly, he was originally created as part of an ad campaign. The

Chicago-based Montgomery Ward department store asked an employee, veteran copywriter Robert May, to come up with a character the store could use in holiday coloring books to pass out at Christmas. As he was good with children's rhymes and limericks, it didn't take long for May to come up with the misfit reindeer story, based somewhat on his own childhood experiences as an outcast in school. (The name Rudolph was actually May's third choice, by the way. First he picked Rollo and Reginald, each of which worked in the rhyme but sounded too upbeat and too English to be used in his final version.)

May's boss didn't think the character would fly. The image of a red nose was closely linked to that of alcoholism, and the last image the department store wanted to push onto little holiday-shopping kids was that of a stumbling drunk pack animal. However, May sent an illustrator down to the local zoo and had him draw up some images of a reindeer, fully equipped with a lightbulb-shaped nose, and his boss was won over.

The character took off, and Montgomery Ward reaped the financial benefits in a big way. Unfortunately, May did not. His wife died of cancer at about the time he was writing the Rudolph story, and not long afterward he found himself in financial trouble and saddled with large medical debts. Since he had created Rudolph on company time, he received no royalties from his brilliant creation. Luckily, though, this isn't another run-of-the-mill company-exploits-employee story. In 1947 Montgomery Ward president Sewell Avery decided to give May the rights to his character. From there, May was able to turn the story into a hugely popular nine-minute cartoon (which played in movie theaters in 1948), the widely known song, and other commercially lucrative incarnations–the most memorable and popular being the stop-camera-motion TV show narrated by Burl Ives. May's money woes were over. Still, seven years after he quit Montgomery Ward to market Rudolph, he returned to the department store and his old job as a copywriter and stayed there until retirement.

Is Santa's reindeer named Donder or Donner?

In Clement Moore's 1822 Christmas poem "A Visit from St. Nicholas," which we call " 'Twas the Night Before Christmas," the reindeer is named Donder, from the Dutch word meaning "thunder." However, in the popular song "Rudolph the Red-Nosed Reindeer," the reindeer is called Donner. *Donner*

means "thunder" in German, so it's not such a terrible gaffe. As a matter of fact, another name in the reindeer lineup has been changed from the original publication. The eighth reindeer, Blitzen, was originally "Blixem." Both Donder and Blixem were directly snatched from the common Dutch phrase *Donder and Blixem!*, meaning "Thunder and lightning!"

Unforgettable Trip

Are elephants still used as transportation in India and other parts of Asia?

Some are, but not nearly as many as in the past. This is primarily because most forests have been cut away, reducing the number of elephants needed for logging–a once dependable job for the beast. Also, motor vehicles are rapidly displacing elephants as transportation in this part of the world. In most countries, the only transporting the remaining elephants do is for the tourist industry, giving rides to foreigners.

Is the African elephant used as a working animal?

Hardly ever. In the Congo, people have had some small success training African forest elephants, but as a rule they are difficult to train, and even then are never fully docile, so the practice never really caught on in other parts of Africa. If you want to train an elephant, stick with the Asian variety.

Do people eat elephant meat?

Historical Horses

Why did Paul Revere have to borrow a horse for his famous ride? Didn't he have a horse of his own?

There's no record of Revere owning a horse at the time, although many argue he probably did. Regardless, he was rowed across the Charles River to Charleston (just north of Boston) to begin the ride, so naturally he had no horse with him. The one he used for his ride was a loaner from Samuel Larkin, a staunch patriot sympathizer. According to the Larkin family geneaology, published over 150 years after the fact in 1930, Brown Beauty was the horse Paul used. Whether this version is accurate or not, we do know that the horse Revere rode was never returned to its rightful owner–it was captured by the British and used to replace a British sergeant's tired horse.

What was George Washington's horse's name?

Washington had several horses throughout the war, but his two prized steeds were Nelson and Blueskin. Mongolia, another favorite horse of Washington's, was a white Arab. A few of his other horses were Samson, Steady, Leonidas, and Traveller, all good and hearty horse names. Washington, however, wasn't so straight-faced when it came to his hounds. Some of his dogs' names were Truelove, Drunkard, Tipler, Sweetlips, Mopsey, Madam Moose, Taster, Searcher, Cloe, Scentwell, Dabster, Forester, Captain, Lady, Rover, Vulcan, and Droner.

Were there any survivors from the U.S. Army in Custer's Last Stand?

Yes, one–Captain Miles Keogh's horse, Comanche, who was found wounded but still breathing. After being rescued and nursed back to health by the U.S. Army, he was put to work trotting in parades and making other heroic public appearances.

Comanche's not the only battle horse we know the name of. Plutarch immortalized Alexander the Great's horse, Bucephalus, when he told the story of how Alexander trained it as a boy. And we know Napoleon's horse Marengo was named after Napoleon's success at the Battle of Marengo. After Napoleon's bitter defeat at Waterloo, the horse was captured by the British and gleefully displayed in parades and such until its death (perhaps from humiliation!). Finally, like Washington (see above), General Robert E. Lee also had a famous horse named Traveller, which is buried next to Lee. Their graves can be found on the campus of Washington and Lee University in Lexington, Virginia.

Why is it called horsepower?

Before there were engines, the only power available in the Western world, besides brute human strength, was the power of a horse. Engineer James Watt coined the term when making improvements to the steam engine in the 1760s. Watt needed to be able to place a value on the energy produced by the mechanical steam engine. The only way that made any sense was by comparing this energy to the energy produced by a team of horses doing the same job–which in this case was pumping water out of coal mines. He hooked up mine horses, one by one, and determined that an average horse could lift 150 pounds of water 220 feet in one minute. This he expressed as 1/33,000 foot-pounds per minute (he multiplied the 150 by the 220), or "one horsepower." A standard was invented that we use even to this day when discussing motors.

There are miniature cats and miniature dogs. How come there are no little horses?

Today ponies and miniature horses are bred for their small stature, but it's true that they're really not *that* small, just small by horse standards. The first horses that roamed the Earth, however, were tiny in comparison to today's miniature varieties. The very first horse on fossil record was the four-toed *hyracotherium* (formerly known as *eohippus*). It had four toes on its front feet and three on its back–like today's guinea pig. As a matter of fact, little hyracotherium wasn't much bigger than a guinea pig, (about the size of your average hare). As the eons passed, this small horse evolved, growing taller and losing toes until it developed hooves during the Pleistocene era. And thank heavens. Where in the world would we have found jockeys to fit the originals?

A Horse Is a Horse of Course

What was the real name of Mr. Ed, TV's talking horse?

His real name was Bamboo Harvester. His voice was not his own, mind you, but one provided by actor Allan "Rocky" Lane. Speaking of talking equines, do you remember Francis the Talking Mule, who was the first talking equine on screen? Hollywood rumor has it that the mule who played the role of Francis was trained in part by cowboy-philosopher Will Rogers. The voice was done first by Chill Wills and then Paul Frees (in the last movie). Although Francis was supposed to be a boy, the real mule was played by a girl mule named Molly.

A Checkered and Striped Past

Can a zebra mate with a horse?

They can, and they do regularly. And not just with horses but with donkeys as well. Zebras and horses are crossbred–usually a zebra stallion with a horse mare–not just for curiosity's sake but because they also make good pack animals. They're usually called a *zorse, zebroid,* or more romantically, *golden zebra.* The names used for donkey/zebra offspring are *zebrass* and *zo-donk;* for pony/zebras, *zony* or *zeony.* Horse enthusiasts who breed zebra mixes would ultimately like to see these mixes allowed into the horse breeders' showring. Although the offspring are smaller than horses, they could easily fit into the donkey and pony categories.

> Where can I hear what a zebra sounds like?

Sounding like a Real Ass

How come a donkey makes the sound **hee-haw?**

The sound would've simply been *haw,* had the donkey not been given an ability not shared by other equines. It can make vocal noises while it inhales as well as while it exhales. This produces the sucking *hee* sound of *hee-haw* that we all know and love . . . or cover our ears and run from.

Why is a male donkey called Jack?

Jack is an altered form of the once overly common name John. When someone wanted to call on the image of everyman, John or Jack would've been the name to use. Hence *lumberjack, jackass, jackrabbit, bootjack, jack-of-all-trades,* etc.

A little more confusing is how the female donkey became known as the jenny ass. Nowadays Jenny is short for Jennifer, but there were few Jennifers hundreds of years ago when "Jenny ass" became Jack's counterpart. It turns out that, back then, the name Jenny was also short for Guinevere–an extremely common English name for girls hundreds of years ago.

Are mules native to America?

No. The mule made it from Europe to America because George Washington developed an interest in the animal. He'd heard that farms throughout Spain were using an amazing work animal that was stronger and more surefooted than either the horse or the donkey. Best of all, it ate less, too. He asked the U.S. ambassador to Spain to inquire further about the animal–the infertile offspring of a jackass and a horse mare–and in 1785 King Charles III of Spain sent Washington a male donkey as a gift. (Washington appropriately named him "Royal Gift.") He was soon so impressed with the abilities of the mule that he began devoting time to its breeding. By the time Washington died fifteen years later, there were fifty-eight working mules on his Mount Vernon plantation, and other farmers throughout the region began siring their own mules from Washington's stock. The mule remained America's favorite plow animal until modern-day tractors were invented in the 20th century.

All Creatures Great AND Tall

They're big,
they're bad,
they're
megafauna,
and they're
some of
the most
fascinating
creatures on
Earth. Ever
wonder how
many
vertebrae it
takes to
support a
giraffe's neck
or how much
excrement
an elephant
generates in
a day? Well,
even if you
haven't, read
on . . . or
Jumbo here
will squash
your head
like a grape.

Me Big Meat Thing

What does megafauna *mean?*

The term comes from the words *mega,* meaning "powerful,
big," and *fauna,* which means "animals." While *megafauna* is
most often used to describe the huge and now extinct Ice Age

creatures like the woolly mammoth or the mastodon, the term can also be applied to the large African and Asian animals which are actual *survivors* of the Ice Age. Why they lived and others didn't is a mystery. For your purposes and ours, *megafauna* simply means "big animals."

But Calling Them Dumbo Tees Them Off

Elephant ears are so huge! Do they really need to be that big to hear?

Not to hear. Yes, elephants have huge, floppy, oversize ears that can be six and a half feet long and nearly as wide. They have several functions, but helping them hear is not one of them. One is to make the elephant look even bigger when it defends or attacks, as if that were necessary. Another is to wave away flies. But the primary use of the elephant's big ears is unexpected: it's to keep the animal cool. Because elephants' ears are thin and rich in blood vessels, heat escapes easily into the air. When elephants wave them around, the blood inside cools by as much as 9° F.

The need for that cooling function is also one of the differentiating features of African versus Asian elephants. African elephants live in a hotter, sunnier climate, and so their ears are bigger.

A Case of Mistaken Identity

Do elephants actually cause the disease elephantitis? Why is it called that?

It's not called elephantitis, it's called *elephantiasis,* and it's not actually a disease in and of itself. It's a condition caused by a malfunctioning lymph system. When the body's lymph system is taxed or not working correctly, it can't effectively fight off bacteria. Sometimes this can lead to swelling in various body parts and a hardening of the skin around these swollen parts. This is where the condition gets its name. The hardened skin resembles the hide of an elephant, therefore: *elephantiasis.*

Elephantiasis is most associated with lymphatic filariasis, a disease that's spread by mosquitoes by way of a parasitic worm that likes hanging out in the lymph glands. When the little worms start having baby worms, the lymph system shuts down. Besides elephantiasis, these parasites can also cause serious kidney damage that can lead to total failure. Most cases of lymphatic filariasis and elephantiasis can be found in Africa and parts of Southeast Asia where populations suffer from perpetual mosquito infestations. The disease can be cured and stopped through a series of community-wide shots, but the shots are costly and time-consuming, because they must be administered annually to be effective.

An Elephant Joke You'd Rather Forget

How can you tell if an elephant's been in your refrigerator?

That's an old one. His footprints are in the butter, or Jell-O, depending on where you were raised. Ba-dum-bum.

King of Obese

What's an elephant's favorite flavor? Peanut?

Not really. Elephants seem to like best sweet stuff of any kind, when they can get it. Unfortunately, elephants are susceptible to tooth decay, so it's a good thing they don't have many sugar-saturated foods to choose from in the wild. Even without excessive sugar in their diets, elephants suffer from natural tooth loss in old age, which often leaves aged elephants unable to eat, resulting in starvation. This natural tooth loss problem has made it crucial for many zoos around the world to crack down on visitors feeding elephants, and to make sure the animals get a good, balanced diet. But if an animal does lose its teeth, it isn't the end of the world–keepers simply change its diet to soft foods.

And Then There Were Three

How many species of elephant are alive today?

For a long time, scientists swore there were only two, the African and the Asian. They believed that the African elephant had two subspecies, the savannah elephant and the forest elephant. However, some scientists doubted that classification. For one thing, forest elephants are smaller than savannah elephants. Furthermore, their heads are lower in relation to their backs, their ears are smaller and rounder, and their tusks are thinner and smaller. After extensive DNA sampling of all three elephant types, scientists concluded there were enough distinct genetic differences between the two African subspecies to warrant giving the forest elephants their own species classification.

Sing Low, Sweet Pachyderm

Besides making loud trumpet noises when danger is present, do elephants talk to each other?

Yes, as a matter of fact they do. Elephants use their trunks to interact socially—something researchers have known for years. However, they've more recently discovered that elephants use low-frequency verbal communication as well. Researchers at Cornell University took recordings of elephant sounds and raised them to frequencies that can be heard by the human ear. They discovered that herds of elephants actually sing to each other.

I've heard of the elephant that paints in the Phoenix zoo. What other arts might pachyderms dabble in?

Music, and not just subsonic singing (see above). It's been known since ancient Roman times that elephants have a keen ear for musical notes. For instance, they follow musical cues—often quite complicated—when working in the circus. Their natural musical ability inspired Richard Lair of the Thai Elephant Conservation Center in Thailand and the neurologist David Sulzer, head of Columbia University's Sulzer Laboratory (who works under the name David Soldier in his musical career), to create the Thai Elephant Orchestra.

The two began by building larger, sturdier versions of Thai instruments–a large gong, drums, a xylophone-type instrument. They added a few other percussion instruments and harmonicas and began training the elephants to play the instruments. They also taught them to follow start and stop cues. At first, the intention was to let the elephants play as they wished, and Sulzer would cut segments for use in his produced pieces. However, the two humans were surprised that the music the elephants made worked as full musical pieces and didn't need any polishing in the studio. The results are more New Agey than show tunes, but not at all what you'd expect from an orchestra with trunks.

Lair and Sulzer discovered that many of the elephants didn't really need to be taught simple start and stop cues; they followed their cues precisely from the get-go. The elephants also seemed to recognize dissonance. When a key on a xylophone was replaced with one that didn't fit the scale, the elephant musician avoided it completely. Eventually she learned to like it by itself, and then she played it over and over again for several pieces. Because of the success of this venture, other elephant orchestras are being formed in various locations. Lair and Sulzer created a CD (with others in the works), the proceeds of which will go to helping raise orphaned young elephants.

Where can I hear an example of elephant music? **Ask**

Pachyderm Party

Why is the elephant the official symbol of the Republican Party?

The symbol started out in 1874 as a cruel joke by political cartoonist Thomas Nast. Four years earlier, by the way, he had revived the equally demeaning Democrat donkey symbol, which was threatening to fade into historic oblivion (decades before, Democrat Andrew Jackson had been compared to an ass, and his party along with him). The elephant idea came to Nast one day when he was in need of a parallel to depict the Republicans' policies, which he viewed as simply random destructiveness. When a news story broke of caged animals breaking free at the New York Zoo, the image of a rampaging elephant to symbolize the Republicans was too good for Nast to pass up.

Despite Nash's negative depictions, both political parties managed to eventually embrace the insulting icons and focus instead on each animal's positive traits.

Watch Out Below!

Is it true that elephants are afraid of mice?

No, that's a myth. As is the one about the "elephants' graveyard," where all pachyderms go to die. The one about them never forgetting is also false, despite their obvious intelligence. Still, Westerners aren't the only ones who've given the elephant attributes that aren't altogether based in reality. The people of India, who live with them and should know better, have come up with some whoppers. The elephant plays a leading role in the Indian creation story: the earth sits on an elephant's head, and when the head moves, an earthquake occurs. Elephants were said to have appeared in the sky at the birth of Buddha–much like the angels' presence at Jesus' birth (the Chinese similarly have dragons flying when Confucius was born). According to the Indians, elephants used to have wings. They can even explain why they don't fly today: One day an elephant was flying and grew tired. Spotting an old banyan tree below, he thought it looked like a good resting place. Although the elephant may have had the power of flight, he clearly lacked an understanding of gravity and physics. As he settled on a banyan branch, it snapped, and he fell below. Unfortunately for him, he fell onto a powerful meditating hermit named Dirghatapas, who was as grouchy as he was powerful. Dirghatapas cursed the oafish winged beast to walk on his legs from that day forward. The wings disappeared, and what was left was the elephant we know and love today.

How did Dr. Seuss come up with the idea of putting an elephant in a tree for his book Horton Hatches the Egg?

More haphazardly than you might think. Theodore Geisel, a.k.a. Dr. Seuss, was drawing one day at his cluttered desk. As fate would have it, he left his window open, and a big gust of wind blew his papers around, plopping an elephant sketch on top of a sketch of a tree. "Hmm . . . What do you suppose that elephant is doing there?" Geisel asked himself. His answer?

"He is hatching an egg." And so the idea was born, and Geisel filled in the gaps with the rest of the story. Geisel admitted later that inspiration never struck again in the same way: "I've left that window open ever since, but it's never happened again."

How much poop does an elephant generate in a day?

The average African forest elephant consumes over 300 pounds of leaves, bushes, and grasses every day. Of that, about 45 percent is fully utilized by the elephant, leaving about 165 pounds of excrement to be dumped on the ground. Now, that's a lot of poop, but luckily it's really good poop. Thanks to the herbaceous elephant diet, the elephant's waste contains lots of seeds that, within the nutrient-rich excrement, germinate well in the African forests. Unfortunately, a decrease in the forest elephant population has resulted in a lack of poop, causing a huge ecological difference. The elephant waste is responsible for a great deal of forest growth, and with less and less of it each year, the forest (and the animals that live therein) have taken a big hit. Yet another reason to work harder at protecting this animal.

General Mistakes

What was it again that Civil War general John Sedgwick said about an elephant, right before he died?

He didn't say anything about an elephant, really. He was talking about the Confederate enemy's inability to hit a target, even a big one. Here's an excerpt from *The Death of General John Sedgwick,* an account recorded by Martin T. McMahon, Brevet Major-General, U.S.V. Chief-of-Staff, Sixth Corps, who was there when it all took place:

> I gave the necessary order to move the troops to the right, and as they rose to execute the movement the enemy opened a sprinkling fire, partly from sharp-shooters. As the bullets whistled by, some of the men dodged. The general said laughingly, "What! What men, dodging this way for single bullets! What will you do when they open fire along the whole line? I am ashamed of you. They couldn't hit an elephant at this distance." A few seconds after, a man who had been

separated from his regiment passed directly in front of the general, and at the same moment a sharp-shooter's bullet passed with a long shrill whistle very close, and the soldier, who was then just in front of the general, dodged to the ground. The general touched him gently with his foot, and said, "Why, my man, I am ashamed of you, dodging that way," and repeated the remark, "They couldn't hit an elephant at this distance." The man rose and saluted and said good-naturedly, "General, I dodged a shell once, and if I hadn't, it would have taken my head off. I believe in dodging." The general laughed and replied, "All right, my man; go to your place." For a third time the same shrill whistle, closing with a dull, heavy stroke, interrupted our talk; when, as I was about to resume, the general's face turned slowly to me, the blood spurting from his left cheek under the eye in a steady stream. He fell in my direction; I was so close to him that my effort to support him failed, and I fell with him.

A Royal Pain

What's the origin of the term white elephant sale?

A white elephant sale isn't just your run-of-the-mill yard sale. It's one in which you sell things that have become a burden but are too valuable to just throw away. The origin of this phrase is this: Albino elephants are quite rare. Legend has it that in Thailand, the white elephant was considered such a find that only the king himself could own one, and no white elephant was to be traded or killed without the consent of his Royal Highness. As you can imagine, however, the upkeep of an elephant isn't easy, and the cost of feeding can run up a pretty steep bill at the local farmers' market. Therefore, the story goes, the Thai king would reserve the white elephant as a gift for only those "friends" he most wanted to get even with. The receiver of such a gift would, no doubt, be initially honored, but it wouldn't take long before he was financially ruined as he tried to maintain the big white beast.

Whether the origin of the phrase is accurate or not, this is exactly what ended up happening to King Charles I of England.

He was presented with an albino elephant from Siam. It being a time when the British king was trying to raise funds, the expense became overwhelming, and Charles suffered great hardship. His wife even had to forfeit her annual trip to Bath that year.

How's the Weather up There?

How many vertebrae does a giraffe have in its neck?

The African plains giraffe–the tallest mammal on earth–has a neck that extends up to eight feet higher than its shoulders. Despite this, it has seven vertebrae in its neck, the exact same number that every other mammal has. Just goes to show you that size doesn't always make a difference.

How does a giraffe get enough blood to its brain, since it has such a long neck?

The giraffe heart is quite a machine. It has to be in order to push against gravity and feed the brain at the top of the giraffe's long neck, which can sometimes be as long as eight feet. A giraffe heart can weigh up to twenty-nine pounds or more, and it pumps three times harder and more efficiently than the human heart.

When a giraffe bends over, does it ever black out?

The giraffe is equipped with an amazing network of veins and valves in the neck that keep blood from ever flowing too fast or too slow, whether the animal is bending over or getting back up. This network has been compared to a sponge: the vessels in the head work simultaneously with valves that partially close to keep the blood from flowing down, and they fill up at a slow rate so the giraffe has time to drink. When they begin to get full, the pressure is felt by the giraffe in time for him to right himself and then the process works in reverse: the veins and valves partially close off, so blood doesn't quickly pour back down into the body. If you watch a giraffe taking a drink, you will see that he doesn't stay down indefinitely, but raises his head now and again.

A Tall Cool One

Why does a giraffe hold its legs out straight to the side when bending to get a drink? To better support the weight of its neck?

That would seem like the logical reason. However, it's been observed that the giraffe's close relative, the okapi–with a normal-size, short neck–also stands with legs splayed, stiff and straight, when it bends down to drink.

With a Tongue like That, He'd Make a Cunning Linguist

How long is a giraffe's tongue?

On average, it's just under two feet long.

How many types of giraffe are there in the world?

There are only two separate species in the family Giraffidae. One is the okapi–also called a forest giraffe–which looks like a cross between a zebra, a mule, and a giraffe. The other is the steppe giraffe, the one we're most familiar with. But there are seven different subspecies of steppe giraffes, including the southern giraffe, and the Masai giraffe. All of these have variations in their markings. That's not saying much, though, because all giraffes, even members of the same subspecies and herd, have variations in their markings. As with humans and their fingerprints, no two giraffes have the same spots.

Lying Down on the Job

I've never seen a giraffe lying down. When do they sleep?

Since an adult giraffe would make a good supper for a lion on the African plain, they've evolved some very interesting sleep patterns. When they sleep deeply, it's only for a few minutes at a time. All of these deep snoozes combined add up to only about thirty minutes of sleep every twenty-four hours. The rest of the time, giraffes may catnap lightly now and again, but their ears are still perked and listening for predators. When a giraffe does lie down for resting, it will usually rest its neck on its rump, a log, or some other prop so that its head always stays elevated.

Welcome to the Real World, Spot Boy

How is a giraffe born?

A giraffe calf is welcomed into this world by experiencing gravity in a most unpleasant way. The five-foot-plus baby giraffe must drop six feet or more from the mother's vaginal opening to the ground before hopping up and trying out its spindly legs.

Where can I see a giraffe being born?

What is the name of the giraffe calf that was born in 2001 at the Smithsonian National Zoo in Washington?

Her name is Jana, which means "large child" or "fine child" in Swahili. Jana was the second girl offspring for Griff. Griff has also birthed four males.

What's the survival rate of a baby giraffe in the wild?

Only about a quarter of all giraffes born in the wild make it to adulthood. This is mostly because they are a favored prey among the big cats and jackals. Although the mother giraffe puts up a pretty good fight to save her baby, the predators usually win the war.

Can't We All Just Get Along?

They aren't white, so why are they called white rhinos?

What's a baby rhinoceros called? A calf.

Scrape off the mud they use to cool themselves, and you'll find that white rhinos are really a dark gray. The name comes from a mistranslation of the Afrikaan *weit,* meaning "wide." This refers to the rhino's wide muzzle, which is specialized for grazing.

Incidentally, the black rhinos suffer from a similar misnaming–they're really the same color as white rhinos.

Bad Day at the Office

Why did absurdist playwright Ionesco choose the rhinoceros for his play Rhinoceros?

In *Rhinoceros,* Berenger watches as the people in his life turn into rhinoceroses, including his coworkers, his best friend, Jean, and his secretary, Daisy. Berenger is left alone to fight all of the rhinoceroses.

In this classic 1959 play that bolstered the playwright's career in America, Engene Ionesco was illustrating his thoughts on the end result of totalitarianism. He was trying to make the point that a government-dominated society turns humans into rampaging beasts, and once it has started, there's no stopping it.

"Heh-Heh. He Said 'Ox'!"

What's the bird that you always see riding on the backs of rhinos?

The oxpecker.

Number Two

Elephants are the biggest, but what's the second biggest land mammal in the world?

Experts disagree on whether it's the white rhinoceros or the hippopotamus. Since the debate rages on, we'll throw in our two cents. On average, the rhinoceros measures taller than the hippo, making it the second largest land animal by height. However, on average, the hippopotamus weighs more, making it the second largest land animal by weight. Does that clear it up?

Two Toes Good, One Toe Bad

Why aren't rhinos in the order Artiodactyla with pigs and hippos?

The order Artiodactyla consists of mammals that have an even number of toes on each hoof. These include sheep, goats, cows, deer, antelope, and giraffes. It doesn't include the rhino because it's an odd-toed hoofed mammal. The rhinoceros belongs to the order Perissodactyla.

So Saith the Lord

What is the behemoth that's mentioned in the Bible?
This one has stumped many a faithful reader. In modern Hebrew, the word translates to "cattle," but it's unlikely this is what the author meant, as cattle are named very specifically in other parts of the Bible. What do we know for sure? For certain, the behemoth was a large beast. Some believe it to be a water buffalo, while still others insist it's an elephant. However, based on the description in the book of Job, it was most likely a hippopotamus. Here's God:

> Behold now, Behemoth which I made as well as you; he eats grass like an ox. . . . Under the lotus plants he lies down, in the covert of the reeds and the marsh. The lotus plants cover him with shade; The willows of the brook surround him. If a river rages, he is not alarmed; He is confident, though the Jordan rushes to his mouth.
>
> –Job 40: 15, 21-23

It goes on to talk about the behemoth's thick, impenetrable hide, his less-than-approachable ways, and his money value among traders. We stopped there before the Lord started making the poor behemoth sound more like an angel of the Apocalypse ("His sneezes flash forth light, and his eyes are like the eyelids of the morning. Out of his mouth go burning torches; sparks of fire leap forth," etc.), which we suppose is what a hippo might look like if you ever tried to pet its snout.

Grunt, Grunt, Chuff, Honk—Pass It On

Do hippos talk?
Yes, they do talk, and not quietly like elephants, but rather loudly. In a series of noises that are called grunts, chuffs, and honks, hippopotamuses yell to communicate with one another or to warn off predators. Their noises have been recorded at

levels of 113 or more decibels. That's about as loud as a jet engine, or a Marilyn Manson concert if you're standing close to the stage.

> **What does a hippopotamus sound like?** *Ask*

How many pounds of teeth are poached from wild hippos?

It's sad, but the poor hippo is bearing the brunt of the effort to save the elephant. Since the United Nations Convention on International Trade in Endangered Species (CITES) officially imposed a ban on ivory trading in 1990, about 30,000 pounds per year of hippo teeth have been exported from Africa. Before the ban, annual numbers were only about 5,600 pounds.

What does the name of the African country Mali mean?

It means "hippopotamus" in the African Bambara language. Its capital, Bamako, means "crocodile river."

Blood, Sweat, and — Well, Other Things

Why is the hippopotamus cage at the zoo always so muddy around the walls? You would think that since hippos are always in the water, they wouldn't be so dirty.

Hippos aren't always in the water, but it's true that they're relatively clean animals. They don't wallow in the mud like their close relative, the pig. What you're seeing on the walls of the hippo cage isn't mud, it's poop. Dominant male hippopotamuses mark their territory by flinging poop with a distinctive finesse. It's an interesting thing to observe: their tails start wildly paddling back and forth as they defecate. This messy behavior is delicately labeled "dung showering" by those who study hippos. People standing nearby, however, call it something else entirely.

Is it true that hippos sweat blood?

No, but it's an understandable misconception based on a glandular condition of the Nile hippo. This aquatic beast has a mucous gland that, when its owner is startled, nervous, or excited, produces an oozing, reddish-tinted liquid that's easily mistaken for blood. The oily liquid normally helps keep the hippo's skin from getting cracked and dry in the hot sun, but the gland's sudden excretions may also serve to scare off potential predators.

Hippos in the Rough

Do hippos ever leave the water?

Each night, under the cover of darkness, hippos wade out of their pools and march as far as six miles in search of food. They circle around and back to their watery beds several times through the night, finally returning to the water right before the sun rises. This nightly feeding ritual is well documented, and in some locations the evidence is hard to miss. Take the Jinja golf course in Uganda, for instance, with its well-kept lawns and manicured greens. The succulent grasses are a huge draw for nearby hippo populations. Hippo tracks are so prevalent that a local club rule was created to accommodate balls that accidentally land in the deep divot of a hippo footprint. It allows a player to lift and drop his or her ball, without incurring a penalty. Don't try to invoke this rule in New Jersey, though; they won't buy it.

Mini Megafauna

Is there just the one kind of hippopotamus in the world?

Actually, there are two kinds: the common hippopotamus and the pygmy hippopotamus. Whereas the common one stands five feet high and is about fourteen feet long, the pygmy hippo is about a yard tall and four and a half feet long. It weighs only about 400 or 500 pounds, as opposed to the male common hippo, which weighs in somewhere between 7,000 and 8,000 pounds. Besides size, the main difference between the two is that pygmy hippos are terrestrial. They live in the underbrush of the African forests and have feet that more closely resemble a pig's than those of the larger hippopotamus. The pygmy hippo's eyes are located on the sides of its head, and its nostrils are flat on its face like those of most land-dwelling herbivores. Its larger cousin, to accommodate its life in the water, has eyes on the top of its head and bulging nostrils so it doesn't have to lift its entire head out of the water to breathe and see.

Primarily due to human encroachment on their habitat, only between 2,000 and 3,000 pygmy hippos are left in the wild. Compare this to the 157,000 common hippos left in the wild–a number that's still too low, due to the poaching of the larger animals' teeth.

Do pygmy hippos live in herds?
No. They're solitary creatures by nature.

Splitting Woolly Hairs

What was the mastodon's favorite food?
Scientists believe it was the fibrous stalks and leaves of the water lily. Many well-preserved mastodon carcasses–too many to make it coincidental–have had remnants of these plants in their stomachs.

What's the difference between a mastodon and a woolly mammoth?
The mammoth and mastodon were closely related to one another. They resembled each other in overall structure, and both looked similar to our modern-day elephant. However, there were differences. The mastodon, for example, had a different tooth structure; its teeth weren't flat like an elephant's teeth, but bumpy or cone-shaped. Perhaps this design was better suited for tearing and grinding up woody or pulpy plants. The mastodon was smaller in stature–about eight to ten feet tall–than the woolly mammoth, which easily stood fourteen feet tall at the shoulder. Mastodon tusks also curved up and were more flat than the mammoth's. Some speculate these flat tusks made good tools for digging out of snow. In contrast, the mammoth had gargantuan tusks that curved down and have been measured at over thirteen feet long. What they were good for, exactly, we're not sure.

Something You Wouldn't Want to Meet in a Dark Alley

What was Elasmotherium?
It was a member of the rhinoceros family back in the days of the Ice Age. *Elasmotherium* means "plate monster." It was huge–

larger, even, than an elephant. Fossils have been found that measure between sixteen and twenty-six feet tall. It's been estimated that its horn measured up to six and a half feet in length, though no actual horn fossil has been found.

Another close cousin of the rhinoceros was the woolly rhinoceros, officially called *Coelodonta antiquitatis*. Like the woolly mammoth, it was covered with long brown hair to protect it from the cold Ice Age climate. It too was bigger than its modern-day rhinoceros cousin; the woolly rhinoceros stood about twelve feet tall and carried two large horns, measuring up to three feet.

Attention: Creativity Dept. of Lucas Productions

The big-toothed kangaroo from the Pleistocene era looks like something straight from a Star Wars *movie. What other strange but true animals lived during the Ice Age?*

Ice Age marsupials from Australia were pretty freaky-looking, for sure. But America had some interesting creatures, too. For example, the giant sloth, which resembled the modern-day tree sloth but was much bigger—about the size of a bull ox—and lived exclusively on the ground. There was also an interesting armadillo creature that was about the size of a VW bug. It was plated like its modern-day cousin, but sported a scary-looking ball of spikes on the end of its tail for protection. The giant beaver, with its six-inch-long teeth, would have been formidable, as would the giant flightless chicken-type bird that had arms instead of wings and was fiercely carnivorous. All of these animals died out at the end of the Pleistocene era, some 10,000 years ago (and none too soon in the case of that chicken), about the same time as the woolly mammoths and mastodons. The reasons for their disappearance are still a mystery, although scientists are looking at several theories, from global warming and asteroids to deadly viruses brought by humans as they began migrating around the globe.

Here, Kitty Kitty!

Cats both big and small are considered the most advanced of the carnivores. You can see why that would be: despite sleeping the lion's share of the day away, big cats can still live fat and happy off the flesh of gazelles and zebras . . . and little cats, off the goodwill of their owners.

Cat Fight

Are tigers hard to breed in captivity?

Actually, they're pretty easygoing about such things. Enough tiger kittens are born in captivity that live captures are no longer necessary to keep zoos and circuses well supplied.

Have lions and tigers ever successfully mated?

In the wild, never. But in big cat refuges in the United States, yes. The babies are called *ligers* and *tigons* (or sometimes, illogically, *tiglons*). A liger is the result of a male lion mating with a tigress, while the tigon (or tiglon) is from a male tiger and a lioness.

Both hybrids are a tawny color with pale stripes, with the tigon's stripes more prominent than the liger's. As far as anyone has figured out so far, these hybrids are incapable of producing young. Maybe that's just as well–the mind boggles at what might happen if they crossed a tigon with a liger.

> Is the lion the biggest of the big cats?
> No, the tiger is.

Orville Redenbacher Runs with the Big Cats

When tigers mark their territories by peeing on trees, can people smell it?

Yes. If you're walking in the jungle, and you suddenly get the sense that you're approaching a movie theater lobby, beware. According to people in the know, trees marked by tigers smell uncannily like buttered popcorn.

Lion groups are called prides. What are tiger groups called?

Nothing, because in order to be called something, they have to exist. Tigers don't group; they're solitary creatures. Even the males and females don't get together except to mate briefly and then move on. Not that tigers are necessarily hostile to each other if they meet at a waterhole or over a carcass. Two tigers meeting on their nightly rounds may even stop and rub heads against each other in the sort of air-kiss greeting that housecats do. But then they go their separate ways.

Do tigers all have the same stripes, or are they different?

They each have a stripe pattern as different and individual as a person's fingerprints.

The Benefits of Being Two-Faced

How do you avoid being attacked by tigers?

Well, if you're *really* worried about it, staying in America and away from zoos and circuses isn't a bad strategy.

On their own turf, tigers can be a real menace—more so, even, than the other big cats. For example, one female tiger in Champawat, India, was blamed for killing at least 436 victims over several years. Even though people, who are bony and not that tasty, do not normally appear on the tiger menu, some tigers are lazy enough to make a meal of us slow-moving humans if we happen to make ourselves available for lunch, especially if they're too sick or disabled to hunt for food they actually like.

In 1987 scientists found an easy, low-cost way of protecting people passing through the swamps and forests of tiger country: a mask worn on the back of the head. Tigers make a habit of stalking and attacking their prey from behind, but if you wear a mask on the back of your head, you don't seem to *have* a behind. Several thousand natives have reported that a backward mask works like a charm: tigers followed them for a while, but became visibly confused and demoralized by the ruse, and ultimately slunk back into the jungle.

The Hazards of Show Business

I saw a white tiger in a zoo and am wondering, How many are there in the wild?

Not many. They're quite rare, and their eye-catching whiteness puts them at a disadvantage when they're trying to sneak up on prey. However, the place where a white coat *would* be an advantage is in a zoo, and more than a hundred white tigers live in various zoos around the world. All of them are the descendants of a white cub that was caught in India in 1951 and given to the National Zoo in Washington, D.C. Unfortunately, the white tigers on display are the result of severe inbreeding of siblings, cousins, and parents mated to their own cubs. This single-minded determination on the part of humans to have a supply of the crowd-pleasing white tigers has resulted in deformities like back problems, hip dislocation, and crossed eyes. Because of these genetic problems, hundreds of cubs have had to be destroyed along the way.

> **Why are Siberian tigers endangered?** **Ask**

If I Can't See It, It Can't Hurt Me

Why is there a difference in the markings of the big cats? If camouflage is the point, aren't spots (like those on leopards) better than stripes (like tigers), and aren't both better than no pattern at all (like lions)?

There's a good reason why different kinds of cats have different kinds of patterns. In forests, with the sun shining through leaves, irregular spots work best to disguise something. Not surprisingly, all of the forest cats, like cheetahs, jaguars, leopards, and ocelots, are spotted.

Tigers can live in a variety of surroundings, from forests to jungles to mangrove swamps, but they mostly hunt in grassy woodlands. Since adult big cats are high on the food chain and are not usually in danger from predators, being perfectly hidden while resting at home isn't as important as being hidden while hunting. Tigers' vertical stripes in tawny colors fit the bill nicely, allowing them to blend in with the tall grasses and woody bushes where they find their prey.

Lions spend all of their hunting time on sun-scorched, arid plains, so their uniformly sandy coloring suits them well. However, their babies, because of their lack of size and strength, are vulnerable to predators. To combat this vulnerability, baby lions have spots for the first year of life, which helps them hide in the shade.

Where is the snow that snow leopards live in?

The Himalayan Mountains of northwestern China and Tibet.

Do all continents have wild cats?
No. Australia and Antarctica have none.

Cat Scans

How much keener is a cat's sense of sight than a human's?

Normally, not keener at all. In fact, except in dim light, humans actually see better than cats. We see more colors, too—cats probably see the world only in shades of gray. Cats see well enough to perceive a movement that's within their pouncing range and beat us handily in their hearing and sense of smell, both of which are especially useful in hunting.

Can cats see in complete darkness?

Not *complete* darkness. Nothing can see without at least a little light. However, cats have a distinct advantage on us in low light. For one thing, their pupils can expand three times wider than ours can. For another, they have a layer of crystalline material behind their retinas that reflects light back out, giving their eyes a second chance to pick up images. This layer, called the *tapetum lucidum,* is also the reason that cats' eyes shine eerily at night when they catch a glint of light.

Unfortunately, what cats gain in night vision they lose in daytime sharpness. While their eyes are perfectly suited to picking up movement, their overall vision is blurry—so much so that if something stops moving, the cat is likely to lose track of it. Which is why you sometimes see cats watching television, but almost never catch them reading a book.

Psychotic . . . or Catatonic?

What is Snookums my cat hearing that I'm not? Or is she just psychotic?

She is no more psychotic than most house cats, we'd wager. It's true, though, that Snookums likely hears a lot more than you do. The highest frequency people can hear is in the low 20,000 vibrations per second. Cats can hear frequencies as high as 70,000. They also have ears that move independently to help them pick out the exact location of sounds—the better for little Snookums to track them little mousies . . . or a can opener being operated somewhere in the distance.

Cat's Kills

Would house cats eat their owners if the owners died and the cats got hungry?

Are you a cat owner? Do you really want to know? If not, skip to the next question, and we'll meet you down there in a second.

Okay, then: as you know, there have been dozens of stories of loyal dogs standing guard over their owners' bodies, disregarding their own hunger and thirst as they carry on their lonely, sad vigil. Funny thing, though, we haven't heard many stories of cats doing the same thing.

We know that big cats in the wild are opportunists, eating whatever they can catch, find, or steal, but what about the little one sleeping on your lap right now? Yep, the cats in your house are not that different. While a dog will normally wait until it is very hungry–a couple of days or more–before feeding on its beloved owner, a hungry cat may well decide that you'll do as a protein source before your body has even grown cold. After all, you provided them with food all those years while you were still living, so why not after?

It's their nature. They can't help it. Still, it's yet another reason to keep an eye on the little beasts. As one forensics expert put it: "On those lazy afternoons when your cat is lying there on the sofa watching you with half-closed eyes, it's likely thinking about lunch and checking to see if your chest is still moving up and down."

Just Lion Around

How many hours a day does a lion lounge around, resting?

About the same as little Snookums, the house cat–about twenty to twenty-two hours a day. Lions spend the rest of the time looking for food–either by hunting, by scavenging things that have died from disease or other natural causes, or by stealing food from hyenas and vultures. Since they spend so little time hunting, they often aren't successful in finding food. As a result, the life of a lion is a matter of feast or famine–going several days without food, and then gorging itself when it can. A male lion can eat 75 to 90 pounds in one sitting, meaning that a 600-pound zebra won't necessarily satiate every member in a pride (ten to thirty-five lions).

Can lions climb trees?

They can, but they rarely are inspired to do so. Unlike some other cats, lions don't lie in trees waiting for unsuspecting prey to come tripping along below. Lions seem to climb trees only when they want to escape from the heat or need to get out of the way of an oncoming stampede.

How long have people been training lions?

Although lions aren't exactly the most cooperative animals, people have been training them since nearly the beginning of recorded history. The annals say that the Egyptian pharoah Ramses II (1290 to 1224 B.C.) had a tame lion that he took into battle as a mascot, and the Roman emperor Elagabalus (A.D. 218-222) paraded in a chariot that was pulled by lions. The secret to training lions (or house cats, for that matter) is to work with great patience and without cruelty, always remembering that they're never completely tame–they always have the potential to attack with little or no warning. As a result of this unpredictability, lion trainers who get too comfortable around their felines often end up mauled or even killed.

Does the population of a lion pride change, or is it pretty stable?

If you're a female lion, it's pretty stable in that you can always come home and they'll let you in. Multiple generations of lionesses live in one pride, rarely leaving (although individuals sometimes split off into smaller groups and recombine later).

However, if you're a male lion, don't expect that you'll always have a place in the old pride. In fact, male cubs are forcibly chased away by Daddy at age two or three. They are forced to wander alone until they are fully grown and sexually mature at about age five. That's when they get their full manes and strength, and that's when they become ready to try to take over a pride from another lion, either individually or in coalition with some brothers or trusted associates.

Try is the operative word here. Many young males don't manage to succeed, and some are either severely injured or killed in the attempt. The ones that don't succeed in capturing a pride can spend the rest of their lives wandering nomadically. Even those males that manage a victory find that the triumph can be less than expected. They usually end up leaving the pride within a few months to a few years, either being forced out by other male lions or simply choosing to abandon that position for the nomadic life once again.

Do lions adopt each other's cubs?

Cubs belong to the pride, and they're well taken care of and protected. Cubs can go to any nursing lioness within the pride and be assured of milk. The bad news is that adult males outside the pride are not so kind. When a new male or coalition takes over a pride, their first order of business is to kill all the young cubs. Although it seems cruel, their grip on power is so short that if they don't, they may not have a chance to reproduce before they themselves are dethroned. Some mothers try to defend their cubs, a few successfully, some suffering great injury or death as a result.

On the other hand, lion moms aren't completely angelic or self-sacrificing. All go into heat again within a few weeks of their cub's death, with most becoming pregnant again within four to five months. And if there's a shortage of food, mother lions don't go hungry–they eat first, and if there's not enough food for their offspring, they abandon them to be killed by predators or starve.

Laying It on the Lion

How often do lions mate?

Lions are polygamous, and in the wild a female will normally breed every two years. During the female's estrous period, the male and the female mate once every twenty minutes, day and night, for up to five days.

Why do male lions have manes, but females don't?

It's the males that do the fighting. The mane makes the lion look bigger and more intimidating, and it softens the powerful blows of the other lion's paws. The bad part of the ostentatious mane is that it makes it harder for the lion to successfully sneak up on prey when hunting. Luckily, the females do the lion's share of the hunting, anyway.

Catcalling

What's the difference between panthers and leopards?

None. They're the same animal. They come with a gradation of colors, so some people tend to call darker ones panthers. There's a lot of that with cat names. For example, the puma is also known as the cougar, the mountain lion, and the catamount, as well as a half-dozen other names. It just goes to show you that it doesn't matter what you call a cat, it still won't respond.

What is the most common nickname of college football teams in the United States?

The Tigers. Felines do very well in the NCAA. Cat nicknames like the Tigers, Cougars, Lions, and Pumas outnumber dog nicknames like Bulldogs, Terriers, Wolves, and Huskies by more than two to one.

Tiger, Tiger, Burning Bright

What's a "tiger box" in Japan?

The drunk tank in a police station.

Where can I find live web cams of big cats in the wild?

The Truth about Cats & Gods

Why did the Egyptians worship cats?

Egyptians discovered very early that cats, though not particularly loyal, at least had the virtue of being useful. By catching rodents, cats protected the food supply. Egyptians also used cats as retrievers in bird hunting–their owners would stun birds with boomerangs and unleash the cats to finish them off and bring them back. Egyptians thought that a cat in the house ensured that the household would have many children because the cat-headed Bastet was the goddess of love and fertility. Cats were respected enough to be mummified with their owners or buried in special cat-god fields, and it was against the law to take them out of Egypt (not that the law did much good–Phoenician sailors smuggled them out of the country and traded them around the Mediterranean).

Has any other group besides the Egyptians worshiped cats as gods?

The way we pamper cats, you could make a case that modern Americans do. In addition, though, you'll find cat-based religions in past or present Thailand (Siam), China, India, and among the Incas in South America.

It may be hard to believe, but the Bible doesn't mention cats of any sort, not even once. However, a part of the Talmud written in about A.D. 500 waxes eloquent about cats' admirable qualities, encouraging believers to own cats "to help keep their houses clean."

Where did Felix the Cat get his name?

It was a little joke based on *Felis catus,* the Latin name for the common house cat.

What were house cats before they were domesticated?

Cat-thropologists, if we can call them that, believe that the modern cat comes from two different sources. The shorthaired breeds were descended from a species of African wildcat called the Caffre cat *(Felis libyca).* Tamed by the ancient Egyptians sometime around 2500 B.C., the Caffre was brought back to Europe by the Crusaders, where it bred with small indigenous wildcats, and the modern house cat was formed. The longhaired cats, on the other hand, seem to have descended from the Asian wildcat *(Felis manul).* Both kinds of cat stabilized in size and shape centuries ago and have preserved their independent attitude and proclivity for solitary hunting. Good thing, too. Would any animal alive be able to defend itself against a determined pack of house cats? Not likely!

What's the difference in life span between your average indoor cat and outdoor cat?

Cats live hard and die fast outside in the modern world. Not only do they have to worry about other cats, dogs, and wild animals, but they also have a bigger menace to face: the Jaguars, Cougars, Lynxes, Vipers, Rams, Impalas, and Mustangs that speed along our roads. Getting down to specifics, the Animal Rescue Foundation estimates that outdoor cats live an average of three years; indoor/outdoor cats, seven years; and indoor-only cats, fifteen to eighteen years.

Political Animal

Are Siamese cats really from Siam? When did they first come to America?

Yes, Siamese cats originated in Siam, now known as Thailand. The first American to own one was reportedly Lucy Hayes, wife of President Rutherford B. Hayes, in the 1870s. The cat was a present from David Sickels, the ambassador to Siam. Mrs. Hayes named it, sensibly enough, Siam.

A mere Siamese cat wasn't the most exotic feline in the White House: Teddy Roosevelt kept a lion; Martin Van Buren, a pair of tiger cubs; and Calvin Coolidge, a bobcat named Smokey.

Don't Bother Calling the Fire Department

Most cats climb trees, and some can even figure out how to get down again without help. Does any kind of cat actually live in trees?

The margay of South and Central America spends nearly all of its time in trees, only rarely coming down to the rain-forest floor below. Not surprisingly, the margay has evolved to the point that it eats mostly birds, tree-dwelling mammals, and reptiles, instead of the usual ground-ranging fare. It's so well adapted that it can even turn its rear feet backward and hang like a squirrel while descending a branch.

Missing Lynx

Do any lynxes live in the United States?

Yes. Two of the four species of the lynx family are native to the United States. It's confusing because one of them is popularly called the Canadian lynx and the other, the bobcat or wildcat. The other two, non-American lynxes are the Spanish lynx and the Eurasian lynx.

Making Like a Catamaran

Do any cats like water?

You may already know that most cats *can* swim, they just would strongly prefer not to. The jaguarundi, on the other hand, likes swimming so much it's sometimes called the otter cat. Found in a range from Arizona and Texas to Argentina, it prefers living near water, where it can dive in now and again for a fish or a frog. Tigers and jaguars are also willing to swim, although not as enthusiastically as the jaguarundi.

Come Out and Play with Me

It's pretty gruesome how cats play their prey to death. Do all felines do that?

No, most are fairly quick about killing so they can get on with the serious business of eating. A feline's typical method of catching a big animal is to hold on with its claws while clamping its jaws around the prey's neck to quickly break its spinal cord and/or suffocate it (smaller victims usually get just a mouth on the head that crushes their skulls). A quick kill makes sense. Why, after all, would a big cat want to waste energy catching and recatching its prey?

Of course, not all cats follow the method that makes the most sense. Take the serval, a large wildcat that lives in southern Africa, for instance. When hunting, a serval acts like a house cat, playing with its prey, releasing it, and catching it again. Perhaps, like a house cat, it doesn't need to worry about going hungry, so it can afford to risk letting some food escape simply for the joy of the game. Servals are, after all, compact enough that they don't require the same huge quantities of food as the big cats. More significant, they're devastatingly effective at hunting. Even at full speed, they can change directions on a dime and leap ten feet into the air, landing on their victims with both front paws. Statistics kept by researchers tell the story of their effectiveness: servals successfully catch an animal on 40 percent of their pounces during the day and 59 percent of their pounces during the night. With a success rate like that, you can afford to risk having a little sadistic fun.

Cheetahs Never Prosper

What's the oldest existing type of big cat?

Before any of the other big cats, there was the cheetah, which originated about 4 million years ago. The oldest cheetah fossils have been uncovered in what is now Nevada, Texas, and Wyoming. Until the end of the last Ice Age (about 10,000 years ago), cheetahs were common in North America, Asia, Africa, and Europe.

Are cheetahs an endangered species?

Yes. Although they're capable of zooming along at freeway speeds (up to 71 mph), even the fastest land animal on Earth can't outrun the effects of sharing the world with humans. Cheetahs are nearly extinct in Asia, Libya, and India, where they were once trained by humans as hunting animals, and they are officially endangered in tropical Africa.

Where can I learn which other species are listed as endangered?

Do all cats have retractable claws?

Almost all of them do. The cheetah is the only one that doesn't sport a set–its claws are always out. Cheetahs also have the distinction of being one of the most genetically uniform animals. All cheetahs have the same blood type, and any of them can accept a skin graft or organ donation from any other.

What does cheetah mean?

It's Hindi for "spotted one."

Where can I download a sound file of a cheetah's roar?

You can't. There's no such thing, since cheetahs don't roar. They do, however, purr like a kitten, hiss, whine, and growl. And when they want to deliberately draw attention to themselves, they make a birdlike chirping sound.

Fast Food

What do cheetahs eat?

Mostly gazelles, which are also known for their speed. They watch for one that has strayed from the herd. The cheetah tries to sneak within 50 yards of its prey before attacking, since a cheetah can go its top speed for only about 300 yards. If the gazelle manages to escape capture for that distance (and most do), the cheetah gives up and skulks off to try again. When desperate, cheetahs will also occasionally eat impalas, birds, rabbits, and the babies of animals like the warthog, kudu, sable, and oryx. They not only catch food fast, they eat it as fast as they can as well. That's because they're not that good at self-defense– if challenged for their food by lions, hyenas, jackals, or other opportunists, the cheetahs will most often lose.

Man's Best Friend

There's no denying the strong bond between human and canine. Mark Twain once said, "Heaven goes by favor. If it went by merit, you would stay out and your dog would go in." What Twain failed to realize, however, is that your loyal dog is just doing what it has to do, by nature, to survive: fit in with its pack.

Doggy Styles

How many breeds of dog does the American Kennel Club recognize in dog competitions?

The AKC recognizes 150 breeds of dog in seven main categories. *Sporting dogs* (setters and the like) are used to hunt animals.

Hounds (bassets, dachshunds, greyhounds, and beagles) are used to aid hunters with their keen eyesight and sense of smell. *Working dogs* (St. Bernards, boxers, and Great Danes) are bred to rescue, guard, and lug things around. *Terriers* (Scotties, Airedales, and Cairn terriers) are the largest group of dogs. These were initially bred to get rid of pests like rats and mice—perhaps as a cat substitute during the Middle Ages, when cats were viewed as satanic. *Toy* dogs (like the Chihuahua and the miniature poodle) are in existence simply as showpieces. Traditionally, they've been the pets of the royal and rich. Members of the ambiguous group of *nonsporting dogs* (for example, dalmatians and chows) have various characteristics of sporting dogs but don't fit under any specific classification. Lastly, *herding* dogs (like German shepherds, Old English sheepdogs, and collies) were bred only to herd livestock. A separate *miscellaneous* category exists in some dog shows for breeds that aren't yet officially accepted for registration but are growing in popularity among breeders.

What breed of dog is Toto in The Wizard of Oz?
A Cairn terrier.

What breed of dog is Snoopy?
A beagle.

For Dog & Country

When did the American foxhound breed originate?
It's a mix of English hounds that were brought to the United States in 1650, and a French hound that was given as a present to President George Washington. Washington is credited with introducing to America not only this classic hunting dog, but also the mule (see page 121).

What does "Best in Show" mean?
At each AKC-sanctioned dog show, the judges choose a winner for each of the seven categories (sometimes extra categories are included at the discretion of the promoter). Each of those winners competes against the others on overall appearance and show-manship. The one that wins among the winners is honored with the title Best in Show.

Where can I find a synopsis of the satirical movie *Best in Show?*

Give Us This Day Our Doggie, Bred

How long have people been breeding dogs?

Domestication occurred at least 10,000 years ago, and evidence of the oldest known breed–the saluki, a Middle Eastern dog– appeared on artifacts as long ago as 7000 B.C. Ancient Egyptians were breeding hunting dogs that resembled large mastiffs before 1500 B.C. The irresistible, fluffy Maltese also dates back to ancient Egypt, around 500 B.C. They were worshiped as gods alongside members of the royal family.

In contrast, the Chihuahua was possibly bred as a mere hand warmer for Aztec royals in drafty palaces. The little dogs could easily fit inside the sleeves of robes, and their body temperatures may have kept the hands of the kings, queens, princes, and princesses from getting cold while they did their royal duties. Priests also used them as afterlife amulets for the dead; their presence was believed to ward off evil spirits, so they were sacrificed in burial rituals. Ordinary Aztec people, however, kept them as house pets and for food.

That Frasier *dog Eddie is so cute! Who is the Jack Russell that the Jack Russell terrier is named after?*

Eddie, and all other Jack Russell terriers, descended from dogs bred for hunting in the 1800s using traditional fox terriers. (Most historians say the pre-1900 fox terrier very much resembles what we see today as the Jack Russell.) The Jack Russell got its name from the man who originally bred it: the Reverend John ("Jack") Russell.

As old as this English breed is, it was only recently recognized by the AKC–in 1997. We're assuming Eddie (whose real name, by the way, is Moose) can be thanked for placing this breed in the spotlight.

The dog looks nothing like a bull, so why is it called a bulldog?

Bulldogs were so named because they were especially bred for bull baiting. This was a "sport" in which a bull was chained to a pole, and dogs were let loose to tear the bull to bits while spectators watched and cheered.

The sport was made illegal in 1835, and breeders began breeding the traits of viciousness and fearlessness from these dogs so the breed could live on as house pets. It was a success, and you can now trust that they'll be sweet to your family members . . . and even to your bulls.

What's a Staffordshire terrier?
That was what the AKC called the American pit bull until 1936.

What does shar-pei mean?
The name of this rare, wrinkly-skinned Chinese dog comes from the Chinese *shar-pei,* "sharkskin."

Hair of the Dog

Did St. Bernard dogs really save lives in the Alps?
Yes, they did. By the best count, they've saved more than 2,500 lives over the last 200 years alone. The man behind the mission was an Italian clergyman named Bernard. During the Middle Ages, he founded a hospice in Valle d'Aosta on the border of Switzerland and Italy, and added the famous doggy search-and-rescue mission. The hospice is still operating there, and the big furry dogs are still bred in a kennel out back. These days, however, they're kept more for sentimental reasons than for rescue, since cars and helicopters are now more effective at rescuing stranded people than big sloppy dogs. In case you were wondering, the St. Bernard rescue dogs really did wear casks of brandy on their collars. It gave the people they found an illusion of being a little warmer until real help arrived.

Arf Wits

Which is smarter, a cat or a dog?
Intelligence is not easy to measure even within a single species like ours, which is able to communicate and willing to sit through IQ tests. It's even harder when judging between species. What tests would you put each species through? For example, when comparing cats and dogs, it's true that a dog is easier to train, which might be thought of as an indicator of intelligence. But there's an evolutionary reason for this: dogs are highly social animals, dependent on finding a place within their social structure for survival. Cats, on the other hand, are solitary and don't need other cats to survive, so they have no evolutionary need to follow our lead. This doesn't make the dog

smarter, or the cat dumber; it simply indicates a difference in what is required of them. Both are equally suited to the lives they lead.

Okay, then, which breed of dog is the smartest?

Dogs were bred for specific functions, making intelligence a hard thing to compare among them as well. For example, if you see herding ability as a sign of intelligence, a collie will beat a beagle any day. But if tracking is your sign of smarts, then the collie will lose to the beagle. That said, however, some neuropsychologists insist there are different levels of intelligence despite instincts and breeding. They've developed IQ tests for dogs to measure both their instinctual intelligence and their problem-solving intelligence. There's also a specialized working/obedience intelligence test that researchers calibrate depending on which breed is being tested.

According to Stanley Coren, author of *The Intelligence of Dogs*, 79 of the 150 breeds have been put through these IQ tests (and no, we don't know why all were not included). The top ten most intelligent breeds are almost exclusively classified as either herding or working dogs. The ten least intelligent include a large number of hounds and toys.

The ten most intelligent breeds are Border collie, poodle, German shepherd, golden retriever, Doberman pinscher, Shetland sheepdog, Labrador retriever, papillon, rottweiler, and Australian cattle dog. The ten least intelligent breeds are shih tzu, basset hound, mastiff, beagle, Pekingese, bloodhound, borzoi, chow chow, bulldog, basenji, and Afghan hound.

His Tale Cut Short and His Years Cut Long

Do dogs age seven years to every one of our human years? Is my three-year-old dog actually twenty-one in dog years?

Not exactly. The seven-to-one ratio was just an average figured by comparing human life expectancy with dog life expectancy. Here's how it more accurately breaks down: the first year of a dog's life is equal to about nineteen or twenty human years, give or take a few years. In that first year, the dog will go through infancy, young childhood, puberty, and the rebellious teen years. By the time it hits its second year, your dog is a young adult. From that point on, you can fairly figure that a human year equals about four dog years.

Do dogs have belly buttons?

Yes, like all mammals, dogs have belly buttons. However, if you have the chance to look (and a canine that is willing to let you), you won't find one that looks like ours. It looks more like a line or a scar, and it is, in most cases, covered with more hair.

Stupid Dog Tricks

Why do dogs scratch with their hind legs when they're rubbed on their side?

Because they're being tickled, in a sense. They do this in the same way that your arms flail and you jerk away when someone pokes you in the ribs, or your leg kicks when the doctor knocks your knee. A dog's central nervous system translates your touch as an irritant—a flea or tick, let's say. The dog is instinctually responding by scratching at it. Knowing this, we can't imagine this game would be much fun for the dog, despite the hours of entertainment it may provide its owner.

Scumber Party

Is there a name for dog dung, or do I have to be rude and actually use the word poop in polite company?

Believe it or not, there is a precise word for the poop that domesticated dogs leave behind. It's called *scumber*, which we think sounds much, much better than *poop*. If you're speaking of wild dog poop, though, like that of a wolf or jackal, the word used is *lesses*. *Lesses* is also used to denote wild boar or bear dung.

My dog has a new litter of puppies. She always seems to be cleaning them—particularly their bottoms. I've not seen any evidence they're going to the bathroom, so why does she keep cleaning them there all the time?

Ew, we're not sure you really want to know this one. Puppies are completely helpless at birth—even more so than human babies.

They're not able to hear for two to three weeks because their ear canals remain sealed. They don't even open their eyes for at least ten days, and sometimes longer. Since it's not easy being a newborn pup, Mom tries to make things easier. She makes sure they all stay in a pile together and don't wander too far. She makes her milk available almost all the time.

This motherly devotion goes even further. The puppies can't go to the bathroom at all, even though they're consuming milk, so she licks their hind ends to help stimulate them to empty their bladders and bowels. The reason you don't see any evidence that the puppies are eliminating waste is because their mother consumes it while she's licking. As we said, "Ew!"

This stage doesn't last too long. Suddenly, about three weeks into life, the little dogs can jump up, see, hear, bark, wag their tails, romp, and play. And they're able to go potty all by themselves, too. Oh, how you'll long for those first few weeks then!

Chocolate to Die For

Yeah, yeah, we all know chocolate and dogs don't mix. So give it to me straight, Jeeves, how bad will it really hurt Fido if I share my Easter stash with him?

It's bad. However, how bad depends on the quality and quantity of the chocolate, and the size of your dog. First, some chocolate basics. The active ingredient in chocolate is a caffeine-related chemical called *theobromine.* The darker the chocolate, and/or the higher the quality, the more theobromine you'll find there. For instance, a Kit Kat bar—a wafer cookie lightly coated in low-octane milk chocolate—doesn't have as much theobromine as a square of unsweetened baker's chocolate or a dark chocolate Godiva truffle. Because dogs (and other animals as well) metabolize theobromine more slowly than humans, this chemical can be highly toxic to them. The small milk chocolate Easter egg you have in your basket might not have enough theobromine to kill Fido, although the amount of chocolate a dog can consume without ill effects depends on its weight. If Fido weighs 110 pounds and eats a pound of M&Ms, he'll probably live—*probably.* However, if Fido's only 60 pounds, and he gets into the bag, watch out. In either case, get your dog medical attention immediately.

It's best, in the long run, to leave the chocolate to the humans in your household, and not even give your pup a taste for it in the first place. If your dog finds your hidden stash, however, here are the early warning signs that your dog has theobromine poisoning: vomiting, incontinence or frequent urination, diarrhea, and muscle spasms. Induce further vomiting if you can and immediately call your vet.

Why do dogs bury bones?

It's their version of a doggy bag; a way to store food for later consumption. It's an instinctual characteristic that's lasted even though the dog has been domesticated.

In the wild, canines like the fox, jackal, and wild dog are often left after the hunt with more food than they can consume at one sitting. Vultures and hyenas are more than willing to relieve them of their leftovers—some even before the pup is through eating. To save the energy of hunting again, they bury what's left for the next meal.

Sight for Poor Eyes

Aren't dogs color-blind? How do people teach Seeing Eye dogs to interpret stoplights?

Forget what you've heard about dog vision. Dogs *can* see color, just not *all* color. Color comes in red, blue, and green spectrums. Canines have a type of color-blindness called *deuteranopia,* meaning they lack the ability to discern the green spectrum. While dogs do recognize some red, it's really the blue spectrum they're best at detecting. This selective color-blindness makes some sense in their world: as meat eaters, green things are just a distraction, a background to what's important to them. They're looking for other dogs and things to eat, so they'd want to see reds and tans, black, gray, and white, and leave the greens to the herbivores.

Still, back to your question: if they don't see greens, yellows, and some reds very well, then how are dogs taught to lead blind people through intersections? That's easy: it's not the color changes that the dog watches for, it's the position of the lights and the changes in the direction of the traffic that signal to the dog when it's safe. For a pedestrian crosswalk, a dog is taught to wait until the bottom light comes on (the one most of us see as green) and cross traffic is stopped before leading its owner across the street.

Who first thought up the idea of dogs leading the blind?

By all indications, it was an unidentified German in the years after World War I, responding to the needs of blind veterans who'd lost their sight during the war. A school to train German shepherds as guide dogs opened in Pottsdam, Germany, but due to lack of funding, it closed its doors not long after. Before it failed, one of its visitors was a wealthy Philadelphian living in Switzerland named Dorothy Harrison Eustis. Intrigued by the idea, she wrote a lengthy piece on the Pottsdam school for the *Saturday Evening Post,* in which she mentioned that she was considering the idea of training her own dogs for the blind.

A blind man named Morris Frank heard about Ms. Eustis's article and immediately started a letter asking if she could train a pooch for him. Tired of depending on others to get around, the Nashville, Tennessee, native wrote that he was eager to see if he could become more self-sufficient by means of a dog companion. Eustis wrote back that he was to come to Switzerland and train with the dog; in return, Frank would return to America and teach other blind people and their dogs.

After training Morris with his new dog, Eustis gave him $10,000 to start his own guide dog training school in Nashville. He called it the Seeing Eye, from a Bible verse: "The seeing eye, the hearing ear; The Lord hath made them both" (Proverbs 20:12). In its first year the school graduated seventeen people and their dogs. The school is now located in New Jersey and still trains dogs and their blind companions.

How much does it cost to train with a Seeing Eye dog?

At the Seeing Eye in New Jersey, the heavily subsidized cost to the student is just $150. According to its website, that price includes just about everything from the dog to boarding and travel expenses. However, a review process selects only good candidates who can care for both the animal and themselves. At the end of the four-week course, the student goes home with a new companion and, hopefully, a new level of independence.

You Sleigh Me

The snow up north sure isn't mushy, so why do they say "Mush!" to sled dogs?

It's not to say "Mush that snow down, boys!" one of the more interesting theories we've heard regarding the origins of the term. Usually people assume that *mush* is an Americanized version of an Inuit word, but it's not. It actually comes from French-speaking trappers and explorers who once used sled dogs to make their way across the frozen Canadian tundra. The word used was *Marchons!* meaning "Let's go! Hurry up!" in French. English speakers heard it as "Mush on!" Eventually, it was shortened to just "Mush!"

What about other directional instructions? To stop the dogs, say, "Whoa!" as if you were driving with a horse. To turn them left, say, "Come haw!" For right, say, "Come gee!"

How fast can a dogsled go?

A good sled with six to eight hardworking dogs should get you blazing through snow in excess of 20 mph.

How much does a good dogsled cost?

Ask

Plus That Wet Dog Smell *Free!*

What's chiengora yarn?

It's dog-hair yarn with a fancy name to conceal its origin. Chiengora has become all the rage among a select group of dog-owning knitters and spinsters everywhere. It's pronounced "she-an gora"–*chien* is "dog" in French; *gora* is short for "angora." Angora, of course, is the name for bunny hair, which chiengora actually resembles in texture.

But dog hair? Is this some weird manifestation of America's twisted obsession with its pets? Well, maybe, but the practice probably began eons ago. There's evidence that old Scandinavian tribes and Navajo Indians are among the ancient civilizations that spun clothing from dog hair. And why not? Dog hair is water resistant, soft, and warm, and comes in a variety of colors from rusty red to jet black. Plus, the dog's been around our homes, shedding wads of its hair all over our chintz sofas twice a year, for at least 10,000 years. If we have to collect the hair anyway, why not put it to good use?

If you're looking to purchase the yarn, however, you may run into a snag. For the most part, chiengora hobbyists spin yarn from their own dogs. For more information on how to do this—and how to get the doggy smell out of the hair before spinning it—see http://www.mdnpd.com/pd/default.htm.

Hollywood Hounds

According to Disney, how many total spots got painted on cartoon dogs for **101 Dalmations?**

6,469,952.

Who was the dog that played Lassie?

The original Lassie that starred in the 1943 movie *Lassie Come Home* was named Pal and was owned by a dog trainer named Rudd Weatherwax. Weatherwax had been training Pal for his owner when the owner confided that he didn't have the funds to pay for the schooling. Weatherwax kept the dog as payment, trained him to act, and auditioned him at the studio. Unfortunately, Pal's white nose streak wasn't up to snuff in breeding circles, so he was cut—although Weatherwax convinced them to keep the dog on as a stunt dog.

One day, Pal's chance to break into the big time arrived. The dog cast in the role of Lassie—an uppity AKC-show-quality collie—refused to perform. She was supposed to swim across a raging river and collapse, near-dead, on the other side. Pal, coaxed only a little by Weatherwax, saw his opportunity and leaped into the rushing waters. The director, Fred M. Wilcox, remarked, "Pal may have gone into the water, but it was Lassie that came out!" Pal got the job, and the rest is history.

Pal was perfect in every sense of the word—he was brilliant in front of the camera, and America fell in love with him onscreen. But like all actors, Pal eventually aged and wasn't able to fulfill his duties on the set. What was Weatherwax going to do? There wasn't just a need for Lassie on the screen—Lassie appearances were raking in big bucks, and this was before the TV show had even begun. Finding several dogs that looked like Lassie was a tall order. AKC show collies lacked the white facial markings and "socks" that Pal sported; there wasn't a large pool of less-than-ideal purebred collies to choose from. Weatherwax decided his best bet was to sire out Pal in the hopes of coming up with at least some pups that had his distinctive markings, coloring, and build.

In the long run, it worked. By the time the TV show hit the airwaves, Weatherwax had seven dogs available to play the role of Lassie. Although Lassie's supposedly a female, all seven were male; all were related in some way to the original Pal and had, for the most part, similar markings. For those that weren't perfect? A little bleach and sock coverings helped hide the imperfections from the camera.

Lassie appearances all over the country still rake in the dough for the Weatherwax family. Lassie lives, my friend, even if she's a distant male descendant of the original.

Dogs of War

Where do Great Danes come from?

Great Scot, man, you don't know? They're originally from Germany. The French gave this Irish wolfhound/English mastiff mix their name, thinking they'd come from Denmark; however, Germans call them *Deutsche Dogges* ("German dogs").

So, what do the Germans call the German shepherd, then?

Deutscher Schaferhund ("German Shepherd hound"). German shepherds were bred from other shepherding breeds late in the 19th century. They are true working dogs, bred not for show but to do sheepherding tasks for humans. Because the breed was so good at following orders, the German military and police started using them, too. In the U.S., they grew in popularity after each of the world wars because American soldiers brought them home from Germany.

Movie dog Rin Tin Tin was one of these, brought back to the U.S. after World War I by army air service corporal Lee Duncan. Rin Tin Tin starred in over twenty-five (mostly silent) films and two multipart serials with the Warner Brothers studios, from his first appearance in *The Man from Hell's River* in 1922 to his death at the ripe old age of sixteen. As with the Lassie legacy, Rin Tin Tin's descendants carry on his name.

Where can I learn more about Rin Tin Tin?

Last Laugh

How closely related are the domestic dog and the hyena?

About as closely related as a dog is to a mongoose.

Although many think the hyena is in the canine family, it's not. Members of the dog family include various wolves, coyotes, foxes, jackals, the dingo, the dhole, and the African hunting dog, as well as many breeds of wild and domesticated dogs. Members of the dog family can mate with one another and produce fertile offspring. However, hyenas are left out of this gene pool party. Zoologists see the hyena as being somewhere between the cat family and the dog family, with its structure being more like the cat than the dog.

Dhig the Dhole

What's a dhole?

A dhole (pronounced "dole," like the pineapple company) is an endangered wild dog from Asia. It's almost extinct and remains relatively unheard of. However, if you're familiar with Rudyard Kipling's *Jungle Book,* you may remember a less-than-desirable character–a dhole named Red Peril. It's one of the unflattering (and untrue) portrayals of this animal that have not been much help in garnering support for its survival.

Dholes travel in well-socialized packs and, like wolves, are totally dependent on the group for survival. Physically, a dhole is about the size of a Border collie, with rusty-colored fur and a bushy black tail. It makes an eerie whistling sound to keep track of its pack. Historically, the dhole lived anywhere between India and Russia and down to Indonesia and Malaysia. Today, few remaining packs survive, and they're difficult to track, so scientists don't know much about their current range or habits.

> Where can I see pictures of a dhole?

Fine Feathered Friends

The world of birds runs the gamut from sweet little songbirds to prehistoric carnivores; from national symbols to the things that poop on your car. Birds have inspired such various creations as symphonies and the urge to fly. Here are just some of the things people ask about them.

And the Bad Mother of the Year Award Goes To . . .

All I've seen of a cuckoo bird is what comes out of a clock. What are real cuckoo birds like?

There are several different types. The American cuckoo is about a foot long and, unlike other birds, has two toes that point forward and two that point backward (most birds have three forward, one back). They feed on furry caterpillars and other insects usually shunned by other birds.

The cuckoo clock, however, was created in the image of the Old World cuckoos. The male's cry is distinctive, and sounds almost exactly like a cuckoo clock's chime. But there's a dark side to the Old World cuckoo. Its other distinguishing characteristic is that the females are parasitic breeders. That means that they lay their eggs in other birds' nests. They lay several eggs in a breeding season, carefully planting them, one at a time, among the other eggs in different species' nests when the mother is away. When the young cuckoo hatches, it busies itself by knocking the unhatched eggs and other newly hatched birds out of the nest. The adoptive mother (always a different species of bird) ends up raising the murderous young cuckoo as her own. It's enough to turn a nature lover bitter and cynical.

Besides cuckoos, do any other birds lay eggs in another mother bird's nest?

The South American black-headed duck, the African honeyguides, and the whydas are also parasitic breeders. The best known to North Americans, however, is the brown-headed cowbird. These birds have actually evolved the capability to mimic the size and color of other birds' eggs. Aiding their survival further, they're well-known song mimics as well. Cowbirds have been raised by at least 206 different species of birds.

Sure, we humans can get sick and tired of raising our own kids—especially after hearing another one of those long, grueling explanations of why Dark Charazard can whip Ancient Mew in a Pokémon battle. But birds, presumably, don't shirk their parenting responsibilities for emotional reasons. So why do these birds do this? It's a matter of simple reproduction, really. When a bird drops off her young in another bird's nest, it frees her up to do a little more hanky-panky, and consequently, more egg-laying.

Where can I see postage stamps commemorating the European cuckoo?

Sealed with a Kiss

I've heard the male hornbill imprisons the nesting female to keep her from leaving. Is that true?

When it's time for the female hornbill to lay her eggs, she finds a hollow in a tree trunk and builds her nest. While she's busy setting up her nest, the male begins sealing up the hole in the tree with mud, bird droppings, and chewed food. He leaves a small hole for her beak, and spends the rest of her roosting time bringing her food and feeding her through this hole. When the chicks hatch, the mother hornbill breaks out of the mud prison and reseals her babies in the tree trunk, leaving, again, a hole through which they may be fed by both parents.

To those who'd jump at the chance to see this as another example of male subjugation, it's only fair to point out that since the mother breaks out as soon as her chicks are hatched, the sealing is probably not strong enough to keep her in against her will. This isn't about subjugation as much as protection: monkeys and tree snakes find hornbill eggs a delightful meal, indeed.

Not Something You'd Want to Meet Up with in a Dark Aerie

What's the fiercest bird of all time?

Phorusrhacos andalgalornis, which lived in South America until about 2 million years ago. Usually called the terror bird, it ranged in height, depending on the species, from three to nine feet tall. Sporting a three-foot-long head, the largest of these birds ran 45 mph and roosted on eggs the size of soccer balls. This terrible carnivore's beak was razor sharp and big enough to swallow many victims whole. Studying it has given us a new respect for our friends, the chickens.

Wins by a Feather

The cheetah's the fastest animal on four legs, but man's the fastest on two, right?

Wrong. The ostrich is the fastest animal on two legs. It can reach speeds of 40 mph, sometimes more.

It's All It's Cracked Up to Be

How big is an ostrich's egg?

About four inches tall and four to five inches wide. There's about as much yolk and egg white in an ostrich egg as in twenty chicken eggs. To hard-boil an ostrich egg would take about forty minutes.

> **Where can I find good quail egg recipes?**

Ethnic Yolks

Are brown eggs healthier than white eggs?

No. That's a myth that started because people assumed that brown foods (breads, sugar, flours) are healthier than white ones. In fact, the fictional James Bond would only eat one type of egg–the one from the Helsumer chicken. Its egg is a dark, chocolaty brown, sometimes described as deep red. They're considered a delicacy and aren't easy to find.

The color of a chicken egg is determined not by diet or good country living but by chicken ethnicity. Chickens with brown feathers and brown earlobes lay brown eggs. Chickens with white feathers and white earlobes lay white ones. That's the most common variation; however, some types of chickens lay spotted eggs, while still others, like the Araucana and the Ameraucanas, lay blue or green eggs. (The earlobe rule doesn't apply here.)

> **What does a chicken's earlobe look like?**

Can you answer once and for all: Which came first, the chicken or the egg?

Many religions would say it was the chicken without hesitation, claiming that their god created the animals and birds complete and without evolution or change. However, evolutionary evidence more strongly supports the egg-first theory. Genetically, chickens can be traced back to an earlier bird found in Indochina called the red jungle fowl. Over time, with enough tawdry little love affairs and subsequent genetic mutations, one of these red jungle fowl mothers laid an egg about 8,000 years ago–the egg that "came first." It produced a bird much more

closely resembling a chicken than a red jungle fowl. So the egg
came first, and shortly afterward the chicken was born,
becoming a fixture on farms everywhere.

Give a Little Thistle

Pieces of hay and grass seem too big for a tiny
hummingbird. What do they use to build their nests?
Spiderwebs and dandelion down, mostly. As fast and small as
the hummingbirds are, you'd think they'd be hard for scientists
to keep track of, but we actually know quite a bit about them. A
nesting hummingbird attaches dandelion thistles to the top
of a tree branch under overhanging leaves, using fine pieces
of spiderweb and sometimes pine tar as an adhesive and
stamping it down with its tiny feet. After the base is done, the
hummingbird starts building the sides using soft down from
plants. To weave these materials together, the bird takes spider
silk in its beak and literally sews in and out, as we do with
thread and cloth. Afterward, she decorates the outside of the
nest with lichen for softness and camouflage. The tiny
hummingbird's nest measures between one and a half and two
inches in diameter and one and a half inches in height; its walls
are usually less than half an inch thick.

Aerie Go Round the Mulberry Bush

How long does it take a bald eagle to build a nest?
It depends on where the eagles are nesting. The bald eagle is
certainly renowned for its large nests—called *aeries* or *eyries*—
which are typically about five feet in diameter. But that's
average. One found in Florida holds the record for the largest
nest ever built: twenty feet deep, nine and a half feet wide, and
weighing close to three tons—equal to the weight of a full-size
car. The bald eagle couple mates for life and often returns to the
same nest year after year to hatch its young, reusing the original
foundation and adding to it each year. As time goes by, their
nest becomes bigger and more elaborate.

The original basic nest can take the pair anywhere between
one and three months to construct. They will usually begin
scouting about three months prior to egg-laying time. In colder

places farther north, some couples build the skeleton of the nest in the early fall before migration so that in the spring, when the weather is warmer and a young eagle's fancy turns to love, they merely have to put on the finishing touches before roosting.

Taking the Plunge

How do bald eagles mate?

Visualize this: High up in the air above the treetops, the two lovers look deep into each other's eyes. They then suddenly twist around, locking their talons together and holding onto each other for dear life as they plummet to Earth, spinning, turning, and diving with wild abandon. At the last minute, right before the moment of impact, they release and soar again, high above the ground. Whew, it's like the overheated prose of a romance novel.

This is how we used to think bald eagles actually copulated–during this plunge, with wild, daredevilish abandon. The truth is, in recent years we've learned this to be false. The plunge is simply a playful flirting game they engage in during the mating season, sort of like human lovers writhing and undulating while dancing in a disco. After this high-flying foreplay, bald eagles go off alone and do what must be done in private.

You Should See Their Little Hair Pieces

Are bald eagles really bald?

No. Bald eagles have white head feathers that contrast with their brown-and-gray body feathers. The word *bald* actually comes from the Old English root *bhel,* meaning "gleaming," or "white," and this is where they got their name.

Fowl Icon

Why is the bald eagle the national symbol of the United States?

The bald eagle was chosen by the Second Continental Congress in 1782 to be the national emblem of the U.S. because the species was unique to North America. Other species were considered, however. Ben Franklin wanted the turkey as the national bird. It, too, was a native American species, but it wasn't just the turkey's positive qualities that lured Ben into supporting it. He simply didn't like the eagle. He felt the bird was of bad moral character. And who can argue with the inherent goodness of the turkey, really? Especially on Thanksgiving. Still, no one seriously considered Franklin's suggestion.

How come Benjamin Franklin didn't like the bald eagle?

The bird is a thug, of sorts, at least when it comes to feeding. Although bald eagles are capable hunters, that's not their first choice for obtaining food, if they can help it. They are what's called *kleptoparasites.* They'd much rather wait around and steal the catches of other animals, like river otters and younger, less experienced eagles, than do the dirty work themselves. Their second choice is to act as scavengers. One of their delicacies is the discarded remains of fish from brown bears. The bears hunt in deeper spawning areas for salmon, feasting heavily on the fatty brains and the eggs to put on weight for the winter. When the brains and eggs have been sucked out, bears throw the salmon remains onto the banks of the river, where bald eagles are waiting to scoop up the leftovers.

If they can't steal or scavenge, eagles will reluctantly resort to the actual hunting of live food. The eagle is a good hunter when it has to be, and has even been seen working in coordination with other eagles, herding fish into shallow waters so all the eagles in the hunting party can eat. This teamwork has only been discovered recently; perhaps if Ben Franklin had seen it, he wouldn't have been so quick to talk up the turkey.

Givin' 'Em the Bird

What's a double eagle in golf?

Double eagle is a term used to denote three under par. This was once called an "albatross," and in some circles it still is. An *eagle* is two under par; a *birdie* is one under.

> What do you call three strikes in a row in bowling?
> A turkey.

Who invented giving someone "the bird," or the middle finger?

Some very impudent individual many years ago, no doubt. By all accounts, the gesture was used in ancient Rome. Caesar Augustus, according to the historian Suetonius, "expelled Pylades [the actor] . . . because when a spectator started to hiss, he called the attention of the whole audience to him with an obscene movement of his middle finger."

Although it's an ancient gesture, the phrase "giving the bird" probably came about during the 19th century, and was born in the English theater. An audience displeased with a performance would break out into howls and hisses in imitation of geese, and display their middle fingers. Most etymologists finger this as the origin of the "bird" name.

Turkey Gobble-De-Goop

Did turkeys come from Turkey?

No. The name came from Europe before America was colonized and was originally applied to the guinea fowl. When European explorers saw an American bird that reminded them of the guinea fowl back home, they called it a turkey as well, and the name stuck. Incidentally, there's a widespread myth that Turkey got its name from the bird (some say the country looks like the outline of a turkey). It isn't true. Chinese records that go back as early as A.D. 500 clearly talk of the Tu-Kues–the ancestors of the Huns. Turkey was the name applied to the Tu-Kues' homeland.

Is it true that turkeys are so stupid they'll look up and drown themselves in a rain storm?

No, that's an old myth. It's true that if you're raising turkeys, they should be kept out of the rain, but not because turkeys stay out there and drown themselves in the deluge, as the old tale has it. The fact that turkeys are often found dead after a heavy shower spawned the vicious slander, and has surely sealed the turkey's reputation as being dumber than a fencepost. But in reality, there *is* a logical explanation for the deaths. Turkeys are naturally endowed with two kinds of feathers–the hard, protective, outer feathers that give the turkey its distinct markings, and the soft, insulating down underneath that keeps the turkey warm. The hard, outer feathers repel water, but younger turkeys lack them. As any camper can tell you, down loses its ability to insulate when it gets wet. Young turkeys in the rain have no means of staying warm and can die from the cold.

Just Getting the Bugs Out

Why was the space shuttle Discovery *delayed from launching in 1995?*

Woodpeckers. Over Memorial Day weekend in June 1995, northern flicker woodpeckers began nesting in *Discovery*'s external tank, unbeknownst to NASA engineers and crew. When the woodpeckers want nests, they drill holes. When the holes—200 of them, some as big as four inches in diameter— were discovered after the long holiday weekend, the shuttle had to be wheeled away to the Vehicle Assembly Building for repairs before launch. Following this unusual event, a team at the Kennedy Space Center called the Bird Investigation Review and Deterrent team, or BIRD (we kid you not), studied the nesting behaviors of the northern flicker woodpecker and developed a plan to repel the fowl intruder.

Something Fowl around the President

Has a pet bird ever lived in the White House?

There have been many presidential birds, and we're not even counting Lyndon Johnson's wife and daughter, Lady Bird and Lynda Bird.

- Martha Washington, although never technically in the White House, owned a parrot that George loathed. Apparently, the feeling was mutual. When George and the parrot found themselves in the same room, each would keep a wary eye on the other.
- Thomas Jefferson kept mockingbirds long before he ever moved into the White House. Once in, however, he had a favorite one that he let fly around the study. Jefferson so loved his bird, it's said he taught it to ride around on his shoulder and take treats from his lips.

- One of the more noble presidential bird stories is that of Louisa Adams, wife of John Quincy Adams. Known at the White House for her silkworms, she also owned a parrot during her husband's term. When British troops set fire to the presidential residence during the War of 1812, she heroically rescued the parrot as the fire was engulfing the White House.
- Andrew Jackson, too, will be forever associated with a bird, but in a slightly more obnoxious way. On the occasion of his inauguration, he bought his wife a parrot as a celebratory gift. The bird was taught many things, including a few choice words from Jackson's earthy vocabulary. As it would happen, the parrot outlived both Jacksons, first Rachel, then Andrew. At Andrew Jackson's funeral, the foul-mouthed parrot let loose a long string of profanities just as the guests were paying their last respects. The bird was quickly removed from the area.

Other presidential birds have included a turkey named Jack owned by Tad Lincoln (Abe's son), gamecocks owned by Jesse Grant (Ulysses' son), canaries and mockingbirds owned by Frances Cleveland (Grover's wife), and William McKinley's beloved Mexican double yellow-headed parrot–a South American species with a bright yellow head. The Teddy Roosevelt-era White House was crawling with pets, including roosters and parrots. Once the president wrote to Joel Chandler Harris (author of the *Uncle Remus* stories) that he wasn't so keen on his son Ted's pet macaw: "Eli is the most gorgeous macaw, with a bill that I think could bite through boiler plate, who crawls all over Ted, and whom I view with dark suspicion."

The Rent Is Dirt Cheap

Where do owls make their nests?
It depends on the owl. Some like trees, others like rafters in barns and attics, and still others make their nests in the ground. Burrowing owls, which live throughout the U.S., from Canada to Florida, usually recycle old, empty animal burrows instead of making their own. They've been known

to inhabit the abandoned burrows of prairie dogs, ground squirrels, skunks, foxes, badgers, yellow-bellied marmots, and the belted kingfisher, and even the occasional drainpipe. After renovating the burrow but before laying their eggs, they line their nests with cow dung to hide their scent from predators.

Another odd characteristic of the burrowing owl is the warning noise its young give off. When threatened in their burrows, they produce a sort of rattling buzz that sounds eerily like a rattlesnake's rattle. Not surprisingly, it does a pretty good job of scaring off predators. But not human encroachment, unfortunately—the burrowing owl population is endangered.

What's in a Name?

Where did the cowboy movie star Hoot Gibson get his name?

Wow, that takes us way back. Born Edmund Richard Gibson, the silent movie star was also known as the Smiling Whirlwind because of his boyish smile and his quick comedic ease on the screen. The nickname Hoot was given to him because of a job early on in his life. In Gibson's own words, "First job I got was on the Postal Telegraph. I was then 15. I rode that for about three months and liked it fairly well. I got a job at the Owl Drug Co., delivering drugs and packages to the different homes throughout southern California or that part of Los Angeles. That is where I got the name of Hoot. It came from Owl and later the boys started calling me Hoot Owl, then it got down to Hoot and Hoot has stuck with me ever since."

> What is a group of owls called? A parliament.

What's the name of the louse that was named after The Far Side's Gary Larson?

Strigiphilus garylarsoni. It's a type of chewing louse that infests only owls. Cartoonist Gary Larson was honored because his comic strip is a favorite among many science folk.

All the Better to See You with, My Dear

Can an owl really turn its head all the way around?

Unlike many birds, an owl has eyes at the front of its head instead of on the sides. While this gives the owl excellent depth perception for hunting, it makes it hard for it to see to the back and sides of its body the way other birds can. To compensate for this, evolution gave the owl the ability to pivot its head so it can check out stuff that's happening on all sides. Its head cannot turn all the way around–360 degrees– because that would cause its head to snap off. But it can pivot its head 180 degrees in either direction, allowing it to scope out all of its area without having to turn its whole body in the process.

If owls have such good eyes for seeing in the dark, how do they keep from hurting their eyes in the daytime?

They've got a natural pair of sunglasses. Owls have large eyes for acute night vision. That's a good thing, because much of their hunting is done at night. However, as you suggest, having large, open pupils for seeing in the dark can pose a problem when the sun is out. So Mother Nature came up with a solution for the owl. It has a thin membrane of an eyelid that serves as a light filter during daylight so the owl can see while its eyes remain protected.

Picking Up Good Vibrations

How is it that a male peacock can make his tail feathers stand on end and vibrate?

It's not his tail feathers that stand on end. The long colorful feathers that stand up are actually part of his wing feather system. Tiny muscles at the base of the quills pull each feather up and make them shake. The feathers bang against one another and create the vibrating sounds he uses to attract female attention. The chicks dig it.

The male peacock doesn't display his feathers when he's frightened, as you might suspect, but when he's courting a pretty little peahen. It's been noted that peacock brains are quite small, though, and the birds are less selective than perhaps they should be. They've been seen, in all their splendid glory, coming on to people, cows, regular chicken hens, and even swine.

Can female peacocks also make their feathers stand on end?
Technically, there are no female peacocks. The birds collectively are *peafowl*, and the females are *peahens*. The peahen cannot raise her feathers. As a matter of fact, she doesn't have much to raise in the first place. Although both sexes of peafowl share a crest of feathers on their heads, the female completely lacks the train of long feathers sported by the male.

Peacocks can't fly, right?
Wrong. Although they're not migratory, peafowl of both sexes can definitely fly. They fly pretty high, actually, and will usually roost in the tops of trees at night for protection in the wild. It would be difficult for them to fly far, though, as their tails would produce too much of a drag for longer flights.

Pretentious Little Group

What do you call a flock of peacocks and peahens?
They're often called a *muster,* although we like the less used phrase: *an ostentation of peafowl.*

Where are peafowl found in the wild?
Today most peafowl are raised in captivity. The two types that we see most often in zoos are the Indian and the Javanese peafowl. Indian peafowl are found in the deep forests of Sri Lanka and India. The Javanese or "jungle" peafowl are native to Malaysia, Java, and Burma. A third species–the Congo peafowl–is native to Africa.

Inspiration Most Fowl

Didn't Mozart compose some of his arrangements based on his pet bird's melodies?
In a way, yes. Mozart kept a starling in his home. While he wrote and played, the starling would sometimes come up with variations of what Mozart was playing. Giving his bird full credit, Mozart would find the bird's contributions appealing

and add them to his composition. When the bird died, Mozart gave it a funeral that included graveside prayers and hymns.

Birds, with their melodic twitters, have inspired a number of the classical composers. One of the most recognizable parts of Beethoven's Fifth Symphony can be directly attributed to a bird's song. Its opening, *ba-ba-ba-BOM,* is taken straight from the mouth of the white-breasted wood wren.

Where can I hear the song of the white-breasted wood wren?

Rockin' & Drinkin' All Night Long
How do those glass drinking birds work?

The kitschy little glass-and-plastic birds that seemingly bob up and down by themselves are fueled by methylene chloride–a paint stripper with a very low boiling point. When you wet the fuzzy head of the bird, evaporation begins on the outside and cools the temperature of the head, decreasing vapor pressure there. This causes the vapor pressure in the abdomen to send the liquid up toward the head, causing the bird's head to dip lower and lower. If you place a glass of water under the bird's head, the head will dunk into the water when it dips down. This slightly warms the head, sending the liquid back to the bird's belly. This begins the process of evaporation that keeps the drinking bird going on and on for hours of endless party fun!

Going Bipolar

From Greenland's Icy Mountains . . .

What makes it possible for plants to survive in polar regions?

For plants to exist in cold regions, they have to be able to survive the cold and then take advantage of the summer sun as

soon as it's possible to do so. For example, many of the shrubs
are evergreens, because not having to grow leaves every year is
a virtue in a place where there isn't much sun. Some have
unusually dark-colored leaves, which helps absorb solar energy
and melt nearby snow. Many have bulbous and swollen roots,
the better to store food reserves in readiness for a quick growth
spurt when the sun shines again. Most arctic flowers are white
or yellow. That's because they're pollinated by flies that see
only in black and white, as opposed to bees that use bright
colors to find flowers.

Do any other animals live in Antarctica besides penguins?

Under the icy waters are huge numbers of whales, but up on the
surface, few things are hardy enough to spend much time on
the frozen land. Even regional plants would likely prefer to live
somewhere else–vegetation on Antarctica is limited to about
350 species of mosses, algae, and lichens. Oh, yeah, mites and
ticks also manage to survive there, as they seem to about
everywhere else, relying on their hosts' body heat as much as
their blood.

No land-based animals live in Antarctica at all, however.
Six species of seals (notably the crab-eater, elephant, and
leopard) emerge from the water once a year to breed (the land
might be cold, but it's predator-free). Only twelve species of
birds live there, of which six are various types of penguins. It is
the nesting place of the wandering albatross, which has the
distinction of having the longest wingspan of all birds–about
eleven feet from tip to tip. The remaining six species are
gull-like seabirds, most notably the skua and the arctic tern,
which divide their time between the two polar regions.

Is the Arctic as barren of life as Antarctica?

No, the Arctic is a lush paradise by comparison. The
temperature is higher, there are more snow-free areas during
the summer, the soil is richer, and the precipitation is heavier.
(Antarctica is, by virtue of its dryness, a desert; the Arctic is
not.) The Arctic has more than 400 species of flowering plants
as well as grasses, herbs, shrubs, and grassy sedges. Birds and
insects are plentiful and frolic during the balmy summer, when
(in some parts anyway) the average high temperature can soar
from well below zero up to a near-tropical 50° F. And of course,

there are the arctic land animals like the polar bear, arctic fox, ermine, arctic wolf, wolverine, walrus, seal, caribou, musk ox, lemming, and arctic hare. And, like the Antarctic, the Arctic has skuas, too.

Not Much, What's Skua with You?

What is a skua?

Glad you asked. The skua is a bird, but it's not a bird you'd want to take home to Mother (unless you don't like her all that much). It is pretty large (measuring about five feet from wingtip to wingtip), more aggressive than almost any other bird, unforgivably mean to cute little penguin chicks, and has habits you wouldn't even want to hear about.

Well, that's never stopped us before, so we'll tell you anyway. As scavengers, skuas clean up seal and sea lion rookeries by swooping down to eat the placentas and excrement that the original occupants left behind. As predators, they eat penguin chicks and rob penguin nests of eggs. Of course, skua defenders will tell you that the penguin populations are not seriously affected by skua incursions, and that penguins likely destroy more skua eggs than vice versa. But who could believe such a thing about something as cute and cuddly as a penguin? Trust us, skuas are just no good.

Goo Goo G' Joob

Why do walruses have those big tusks?

- To fight polar bears, and occasionally each other.
- To pull themselves out of the water and onto an ice floe, where they live.
- Because other walruses think they're sexy.

What are those whiskery things that walruses have? Do they have some practical use?

They're called *vibrissae*. Walruses use these stiff but sensitive whiskers to find shellfish in murky arctic waters. Mom walruses also use them (as well as the rounded part of their tusks) to massage and nuzzle their children lovingly. Although walrus calves can swim within hours after birth, they stay with their mothers for two years, rapidly gaining size and insulating blubber from their mothers' extremely fatty milk.

Do walruses mate on land or in the water?

In the water. Males float patiently near the ice floes, waiting for females to make up their minds and jump in. Cue the romantic music and fade to black. Fifteen months later, a single calf is born.

What does a walrus sound like?

They Taste Just like Arctic Terns

Do polar bears eat penguins?

Polar bears will eat about anything that moves, as well as a lot of things that don't. They probably *would* eat penguins if given a chance. But because the two are poles apart, it just can't happen. We mean that literally: polar bears live in the Arctic near the North Pole, while penguins live in the Antarctic near the South. As a result, polar bears mostly eat seals. Seals, as you may know already, eat penguins. But again, given the geographic distance, the seals in question are completely different species, so penguins and polar bears aren't even connected by a food chain.

Specifically, polar bears especially love the ringed seal. One of their tricks is to hang around ice holes waiting for the seals to come up for air, and then render them unconscious by bopping them across the noggin. Polar bears also like charging the seals' nesting grounds and eating their poor blubbery little babies.

Meanwhile down south, it's hungry leopard seals that eat penguins. They like to swim below thin spots of ice at penguin rookeries watching the black-and-white blotches through the ice above, ready to burst through and grab a bird. Leopard seals can completely consume a penguin in five to ten minutes, or roughly the time it takes to watch an old episode of *Tennessee Tuxedo*. Sea lions and killer whales also like to eat those cute little waddlers. Oh, sometimes nature can be so cruel.

Go North, Young Penguin

Why don't penguins live near the North Pole? If people took them to the Arctic, could they live?

Penguins don't swim to the Arctic because they don't like having to cross through warm water, and they seem to be reasonably happy where they are. However, you'd be surprised how far north they can go. There are colonies in Australia and New Zealand, as well as at the southern tips of South America and Africa. But the surprising thing is that a small colony of a few hundred penguins also exists far afield in the Galapagos Islands, which is pretty close to the equator. The Galapagos penguins probably got washed there by the frigid Humboldt Current, which runs along the western coast of South America; the cold current keeps them happy despite the unbearably tropical climate.

What would happen, though, if we got a cargo ship full of ice and went to Antarctica, filled the ship with penguins, and transported several thousand to the Arctic? Would they survive and thrive?

Scientists say probably not. For one thing, they would have to adapt to a place that contains none of the landmarks they use to establish their breeding grounds and the like. For another, they don't defend themselves and their young well. The reason they thrive so well in the Antarctic is because there are no land-based predators to disrupt their nesting. Odds are that penguins would provide cheap protein to polar bears and arctic wolves for a year or two until their numbers dwindled to the point that they could no longer survive.

Dirty Little Penguin Love

How many times a year does a penguin typically have sex? Once.

Do penguins have a wild, promiscuous sex life like some birds?

No, they mate for life.

Is it true that penguin mothers jump ship after laying eggs, leaving the fathers to raise the chicks alone?

It's true, but to be fair to penguin mothers everywhere, it's not the whole story.

Penguins don't normally spend much time on land, because all of their food is in the water. However, nesting changes the rules. The penguins take to the same land where they were born, colonies of thousands of birds walking single file in the same, often absurdly circuitous route that their forepenguins walked for untold generations. How do we know this? Because the feet of millions of birds have worn penguin paths into the soil, ice, and rocks.

Penguins in warmer regions may dig shallow burrows for nests, but because of the hardness of the earth, Antarctic penguins build nests of pebbles. Emperor or king penguins don't build nests at all. Instead, they balance the eggs on the tops of their feet and keep them warm by covering them with their ample, rolling bellies.

There are exceptions, but typically the schedule goes something like this: in the same way that human lovers are able to tune into each other over the hubbub of a crowded room, the two penguin mates find each other by the sound of their voices. They mate, and the male stakes out a nesting area. He spends weeks defending it from interlopers, as neither parent leaves the nesting area—even to find food. Finally, the eggs come forth. The mother, even more depleted than the father after laying the eggs, makes a rush to the sea to binge-eat, replenishing her famished self and staving off post-ovum depression. The father stays around to keep the eggs warm.

Keeping the eggs at body temperature for the thirty to sixty-five days it takes for incubation (while in Antarctica, mind you) requires extraordinary paternal efforts. For example, the male emperor penguin spends weeks standing stationary for twenty-four hours a day with an egg cradled on his feet in the dead of winter. To keep warm in the minus-40-degree weather, thousands of penguin dads huddle together in a tight group, the penguins on the outside of the crowd rotating in toward the center to share the warmth and keep from freezing.

Shortly before the eggs are supposed to hatch, the prodigal mother penguin returns. She typically takes over the egg tending while her mate takes a long lunch break. He heads back to the sea and replenishes his blubber in a remarkably short time, returning right after the eggs hatch with food for the baby. After that, the parents alternate between taking care of the young and eating.

> Where can I find sound files of penguin rookeries?

Mighty Penguins of the Deep

How big do penguins get?

The emperor penguin stands head and shoulders above your plebeian penguins, towering over all the other sixteen species at four feet and weighing a hundred pounds. Coming up to its knees or so, the little penguin (that's its name as well as its description), or fairy penguin, can barely stretch itself up to a foot and tips the scale at about one and a half pounds. Most of the other species typically grow from one and a half to three feet, and weigh five to fifteen pounds.

What bird can dive the deepest underwater?

Our friend, the penguin. Some species can dive 900 feet underwater–the height of a typical seventy-five-story building–and hold their breath for nearly twenty minutes while swimming.

Could penguins ever fly?

We know it's hard to visualize a flock of penguins flying high overhead, but millions of years ago penguins did in fact fly. Eventually, though, flying became superfluous to their well-being. They didn't have any land-bound natural enemies that would make fast escape by air necessary, and they spent most of their time in the water. Air wings gave way to flipperlike water wings, a change that made penguins able to "fly" through water using the same motion that other birds use to transport themselves through the sky. They swim underwater, averaging about 8 mph (with bursts of up to 25 mph), "dolphining" up into the air every minute or so to breathe.

Right There in Black and White

Where did the penguin get its name?

No one knows for sure, but some linguists speculate that the name comes from the Welsh words *pen* ("head") and *gwyn* ("white").

I read an account of Arctic explorers who claimed to have seen penguins in the northern polar waters. How is that possible?

Actually, the first "penguins" were not what we call penguins. The name was first given to the great auk, a black-and-white bird that lived near the North Pole. Later, when explorers got to

Antarctica, they saw black-and-white birds that reminded them vaguely of the "penguins" of the north, so the explorers called them penguins, too. The southern fowl inherited sole ownership of the name when the last great auk was hunted to extinction in 1944. Well, almost sole ownership–there is also a West Indies pineapple, sometimes used for making a type of wine, that is also known by the name *penguin*.

Are all the auks dead?

The great auks, yes, but twenty-two other species are still alive. Like penguins, their colors tend toward black and white, and they swim with their wings while steering with their feet. Unlike the penguins, they live exclusively in the Arctic and can fly. Notable auks include the puffins, murres, dovekies, and guillemots.

One Good Tern Deserves a Hover

What bird, animal, or fish migrates the farthest in a year?

The arctic tern migrates farther than any other known thing: 22,000 miles each year, flying from the Arctic Circle to Antarctica . . . and then, months later, back again.

Bearable Smell

Do polar bears have a good sense of smell?

Rather good. They can sniff out a dead seal from twelve miles away. Of course, if you've ever smelled a dead seal, that might not seem quite as remarkable as it sounds.

Rip Van Woolly Bear

How do Arctic animals survive the cold?

It's a good question. It gets unbelievably cold, down to an average temperature of 90 degrees below zero, with a windchill factor you wouldn't believe. The strategies that work include lots of thick fur, lots of body fat, small heads, ears, and tails to reduce heat loss, and hibernating through the winter. The arctic woolly bear caterpillar uses a few of those strategies, plus some that the mammals haven't yet figured out.

Above its tiny pink legs, the woolly bear is fuzzy to preserve heat and dark to absorb the sun. That's not so strange. However, what is unusual is that it spends at least fourteen years as a caterpillar before reaching adulthood (it is, in fact, the longest-living caterpillar on Earth). Even stranger, it doesn't bother trying not to freeze, but instead controls the process by manufacturing glycol within its body. What normally would happen when fluids inside cells freeze is that the sharp ice crystals rupture the cell's membranes, killing the cell. Glycol, a type of alcohol sometimes used as an antifreeze for cars, minimizes the size of the crystals and slows down the rate of freezing. The woolly bear's body freezes in a systematic pattern: first the gut, then the blood, and then everything else. However, the glycol spares the cytoplasm inside each cell from actually freezing solid. (Antarctic spiders and beetles also make their own glycol to avoid freezer burn.)

Through its life, the woolly bear freezes and thaws thirteen times without losing its freshness. The hungry little caterpillar is only lively and active during the three weeks of the year right before the summer solstice, soaking up the rays on the frozen tundra, grooming its frizzy hair, eating, and growing a little bit more before going back into its icy tundra bed again. And for what? Eventually it turns into the moth *Arctia caja*, lives for part of the arctic summer, mates, lays eggs, and dies. And so it goes.

Why Rudolph Dims His Light in Canada

What's the difference between a caribou and a reindeer?
There's not a dime's worth of difference. They are the same species, but they're called reindeer in northern Europe because they've been tamed, serving as beasts of burden as well as providing meat and milk (see page 115).

The name *caribou* comes from the French Canadians—it's a corruption of *xalibu*, the Micmac name for the animal. Native Canadians didn't tame them or use them for transportation; instead, they used them in the same way they used other animals like seals, whales, and polar bears—they hunted the caribou and used its marrow for soup, its meat for a main course, its hide for clothing and shelter, its tendons for thread, its bones for needles and knives, and its antlers for fishhooks, spears, and spoons.

THE Petting Zoo

Cattle-Lytic Converter

My teacher says cows can be used as an energy source. How?

Cows naturally produce a gas called methane that can be burned by humans. They release it as they chew, burp, and break wind. A herd of cows can produce up to 450 gallons of the stuff every day. Their dung releases methane as it deteriorates, as well. What's left can be used for rich, nonsmelly fertilizer.

How much water does a cow drink?

A cow can drink about a bathtub of water each day, which includes the moisture it receives from the wet grasses it eats.

If a cow eats onions, will its milk taste bad?

What a cow eats affects not only how much milk it will produce but also how its milk tastes. Dairy farmers are careful to give their milk cows foods that won't make the milk taste bad. Onions are definitely not on their list.

How much milk does a cow produce in its entire career?

In a lifetime, a good dairy cow will produce about 200,000 glasses of milk.

Were there wild cows in America?

Although there were buffalo, America lacked the basic dairy and meat cows that Europeans were used to. It was a good thing, then, that Pilgrims brought cows with them on their long journey. When settlers moved west, however, they were able to outfit their ranches with cattle they found roaming wild–feral cows that had escaped from herds brought to Mexico by Spanish settlers hundreds of years earlier.

What's Jell-O made from?

Besides artificial colors and flavors, gelatin is made from the ground-up and boiled bones and tendons of cows.

Why do crayons smell so good?

Processed beef fat–or tallow–is what gives crayons that distinctive crayon-y smell. Vegetarians can buy Wachsmalstifte crayons, imported from Germany and made with beeswax, or the new soy crayons (from Prang) made with paraffin and soybean oil.

How do you milk a cow?

If you can ignore the potentially lethal kicking legs, milking a cow is easy once you know how:

1. Use a neck harness and a leg harness to keep the cow from kicking–to protect both yourself and your pail of milk.
2. Distract the cow with some fresh hay.

3. Wash the teats with antibacterial soap and pat them dry.
4. Prior to filling the pail, squeeze a little milk out of each teat with your thumb and forefinger. The udder has to be stimulated a little before the cow's milk "lets down," or begins to flow.
5. Curl your forefinger around the teat, and roll downward while pressing against your thumb on the other side of the teat. The movement needs to simulate a calf sucking on the teat.
6. Be patient. If your pail is typical–about five gallons–it will take almost 350 squirts to fill it. With your help, a cow can fill about one of these pails a day.

Got Your Goat

Why will goats eat everything in sight?
They won't. Despite their reputation, goats are not walking garbage cans. They like yummy things, like the rest of us, and wouldn't dream of eating any dirty or rotten food. They do, however, have very sensitive lips that they use to check things out. Short a pair of hands, when a goat happens upon something new, it will often feel a little with its lips to see what it's all about, resulting in the myth that they'll "eat anything."

Do only male goats have beards?
Both male and female goats can have beards . . . not unlike some humans.

Is goat hair used for anything?
Mohair and cashmere are both fancied-up names for material made from goat hair.

Neutered horses are geldings, but what's a neutered goat called?
A neutered goat is called a *wether.*

How rude is it to call someone a butthead?
Pretty rude, but not as rude as your mother may have led you to believe: Goats with horns are officially called buttheads. No, really.

Are goats harder to milk than cows?
While they do have a reputation of being difficult, goats are smaller than cows and like to be around people, making them

easier to milk. A goat also has only two teats on its udder instead of the four that a cow has, cutting the finger work by half. You won't, however, get as much milk from a goat as you do from a cow. Size does matter in these things.

Which type of milk is the most popular worldwide?

Living in a Western culture where cow milk is virtually the only milk consumed, it may surprise you to learn that more people in the world drink goat milk than any other kind. Human milk comes in at third place, especially among the younger set.

Which president had goats in the White House?

Known presidential goat owners include Abraham Lincoln, Rutherford B. Hayes, Benjamin Harrison, and Harry Truman.

Do nanny goats take care of kids?

Although some sheep ranchers keep female milking goats on hand to "nanny" lambs when sheep mothers either die or reject their babies, the name *nanny goat* didn't come from this common practice. In English, Nanny is a derivative of the common name Anne. Like jack and jenny mules, there are billy (short for William) and nanny (Anne) goats.

What did scapegoat originally refer to?

Scapegoat was originally "escape goat," but it somehow got shortened with use. The term refers to a biblical story in Leviticus (16:10), in which God asked for one goat to be sacrificed to him and another, carrying all the sins of the Israelites, to be set free in the desert, thus carrying away all the sins. After that, a goat sacrifice became the traditional ritual of the Hebrew Day of Atonement, or Yom Kippur. Today, symbolic rituals replace the animal sacrifice, but the story is still told.

Do goats live by themselves, in small groups, or in a flock?

Sheep live in flocks; goats live in herds.

Pig in a Poke

Who does Porky Pig's voice?

The unmistakable voice of Porky Pig was originally done by Joe Dougherty, who was a genuine stutterer offscreen, before Mel Blanc took over as the swine's voicebox. Today Bob Bergen is usually the voice behind Porky's "Th-th-th-that's all, folks!"

Why are they called piggy banks?

It was an accidental pun, lost in translation. The banks were originally made from an orange clay called pygg, and were called pygg jars. The similarities in name quickly transformed *pygg* to *piggy*, and the money jars started coming in pig shapes, regardless of what they were made of.

What are pigs used for besides pork and footballs?

Pigskin isn't what footballs are made of anymore. However, pigs are used for a wide variety of products beneficial to humans— particularly in the field of medicine: pigskin, for instance, is placed as bandages on severe burns to protect skin while it grows and heals; the valves from pig arteries can be transplanted into humans with circulatory problems; without pig insulin, diabetics wouldn't be able to control their insulin levels; and research done on pigs led to the invention of the computerized axial tomography (or CAT) scan, which gives doctors a glimpse into the body without actually cutting it open.

Why do pigs like mud so much?

Pigs have no sweat glands. One of the ways they keep cool is by wallowing in the mud. Another reason they wallow is to protect their little pink hides and ears from the scorching sun. The mud dries on their skin, forming a barrier against ultraviolet rays.

How fast can a pig run?

Pigs can run a mile in about seven minutes; faster than most of us. That's about 8.5 mph.

Did the pig from the movie Babe get turned into pork chops?

All forty-eight piglets used in the making of *Babe* were spared the slaughterhouse. The producers have promised the public that they were all given to universities, colleges, and farms with room enough for them to live out their natural lives in peace.

Bah Relief

Are dogs the only animals used to protect sheep?

Llamas and mules are also often kept in sheep pens to scare off predators. Llamas and mules may look soft and cuddly to you, but they have bad tempers and tend to kick hard at marauding wild dogs and wolves.

How many kinds of sheep are there?

There are over 500 different breeds of sheep around the world. Their wool varies according to the breed. The New Zealand Romney sheep, for instance, produces the best wool for making carpet. The merino, in contrast, has soft, fine wool for clothing.

Isn't wool a lot of trouble to grow and shear? Why hasn't it been totally replaced by cotton and synthetics?

Wool is a wonderful material for clothing and blankets. It's warm, and it's soft. It's naturally flame resistant, so it's safer than many other materials used in clothing. And unlike goose down, which many jackets and bedding are filled with, when wool gets wet, it still insulates and keeps the wearer warm.

Besides carpets, furniture, and clothes, what else is wool used for?

Some of the lowest grade of wool is used for felt on pool tables, in shoe insoles, and on piano keys. Other uses for low-grade wool include car insulation, ballet-shoe toe padding, baseball winding, and pads for hazardous waste and oil spills. Because wool can absorb between ten and thirty times its own weight in oil, it is the perfect material for large cleanup tasks.

How much wool yarn comes from one sheep?

A good woolly sheep produces about seven pounds of wool a year. Give or take a pound or two, that's enough to make one nice pinstripe suit.

I saw a picture of sheep grazing on the White House lawn. When and how did this happen?

In our not-so-distant past there were once sheep grazing on the White House lawn. Woodrow Wilson had a flock there during World War I, and sold wool to help raise money for the Red Cross. The Wilsons also kept chickens. No known charity benefited from the coop.

Sheep sure seem dumb. Have human breeders improved their intelligence over the years?

From the looks of things, they may be getting dumber. Examining fossils of ancient sheep, it appears that our sheep today—the domesticated variety—have smaller brains than their earlier, untamed ancestors. It must be the company they keep.

Are catgut-strung tennis rackets really strung with cat guts?

No, catgut was never really made from the guts of cats. And few tennis rackets even use catgut any more. They use a synthetic material–usually nylon. Catgut is actually made out of the small intestine of sheep and horses. We prefer the synthetic; if real catgut is used, it takes the small intestines of eleven sheep to string just one racket.

I heard that sheep owners routinely chop off their sheep's tails. Why?

Sheep are born with very long tails–long enough to reach the ground. When a lamb is born, the owner puts a rubber band tightly around the base of the lamb's tail so that the circulation to the rest of the tail is stopped. In about a week or two, the tail–made mostly of soft cartilage–dies and falls off below the band (an owner will sometimes opt for using a pair of cauterizing scissors for a quicker, albeit more painful, crop). This cropping keeps the lamb's tail from dragging in muck and dung. Apparently, flies like to lay their eggs in mucky sheep tails. Still, it doesn't seem right, somehow.

Final Word on Chickens

How come chickens can't fly?

Just to set the record straight: even though the whole premise behind the movie *Chicken Run* was that chickens can't fly, chickens *can* fly, and sometimes do. What is true is that they can't fly *far.* With their heavy bodies and small wings, they can only go about a hundred yards or so. The record flight of a chicken is about 230 yards–but still, that's farther than an emu, ostrich, penguin, or kiwi can get.

THE Vast Menagerie

As we come toward the end of the book, we've pulled together an assortment of questions and answers for your amusement and edification. Here you'll find—all in on place—the finest collection of assorted animals that didn't quite fit into previous categories.

The Morning Zoo

When did the first zoo open?

Well, let's first define what wasn't a zoo before we answer the question. Since antiquity, it has been common for rulers to have collections of exotic animals in their castles, but that wasn't exactly a zoo. Same thing for the gladiator fights of ancient Rome, for which exotic animals from around the world were brought to be slaughtered for the amusement of the masses. For our purpose, we'll say a zoo is a location that displays live animals for the purpose of public viewing and, with any luck, preservation and education.

Given that, the first real zoo was probably the Imperial Menagerie in Vienna, established for the royalty in 1752 and opened to the public thirteen years later. It started a fad in Europe: the zoo at the Jardin de Plantes (Botanical Garden) of Paris opened in 1793, and the zoo of Regent's Park, London, in 1828.

In the United States, sea captains began transporting wild animals for display in the Americas as early as 1721, when the first camel and African lion arrived in Boston. The first polar bear arrived in 1733, the first orangutan and tiger in 1789, the first ostrich in 1794, and the first elephant in 1796. A near-zoo consisting of a permanent exhibit of live and stuffed wild animals first opened on New York's Wall Street in 1789, long before the bulls and bears took over the area. But the first *real* American zoo, in Chicago's Lincoln Park, didn't open until 1868. The Philadelphia Zoo opened in 1874; Washington, D.C.'s National Zoo opened in 1889, and the International Wildlife Conservation Park, also known as the Bronx Zoo, opened in 1899.

> Where can I see a list of all the zoos in the world?

How Much Ground Would a Groundhog Hog?

If aardvark *means "earth pig," is it related in any way to the groundhog?*

This is one of those questions that we figured we could dispose of quickly with a smart-aleck comment and a quick no.

That was before we did some research. We can still safely say that, no, the two animals are not related; but thanks to a bunch of little-educated Dutch people who were in a position to give ill-informed names to animals, we've had the sarcastic smirk wiped off our faces. It turns out that the *names* of the two animals are very much related, *dank je wel* to those Dutch folks.

When Dutch settlers saw the aardvark in South Africa, they somehow decided that the hole-dwelling animal looked like a pig, so they called it *aard vark* ("earth pig"). When they saw a woodchuck in America, they somehow thought that the squirrelly little marmot also looked like a pig, or maybe they thought it looked like an aardvark. Either way, they decided to call it an aardvark, too.

Eventually, they and the Germans incorporated the animal into a weird ceremony they had performed back in the old country, having to do with whether the animal saw its shadow on Candlemas Day (February 2). English speakers in the United States translated the name of the American aardvark into "groundhog." Unfortunately, some English speakers in South Africa did exactly the same thing in their country as well–they started calling the African aardvark a groundhog (and sometimes, a ground pig).

After more confusion regarding the two animals ensued, practicality prevailed, and most English-speakers now use *aardvark* only for the African animal and *groundhog* only for the American woodchuck (and usually only then in February, calling it a woodchuck the rest of the year).

Is that clear? The animals are not related; their names are related only because those pesky Dutch couldn't tell a pigpen from a hole in the ground. Good. Then let's not get into why the aardvark is also sometimes called the ant bear and the Cape anteater. We figure that if you've got a cool name like *aardvark* getting you into the front of dictionaries, you should probably just stick with it.

What are female woodchucks called?

Not "woodcharlenes," we know that much. Actually, there are old terms to differentiate the sexes of woodchucks (as if such a thing would be easy in the field).

> I have to ask: how much wood would a woodchuck chuck if a woodchuck could chuck wood?

Male woodchucks are called he-chucks; females, she-chucks. Their young are not called kid-chucks, as you might expect–they're called kits or cubs.

Not to Be Confused with Peccadillos

What does armadillo *mean?*

The animal was named by Spanish Conquistadors, and it means "little man in armor." If you want to pronounce the Spanish word correctly, you should not say "arm-a-dill-o" but "arm-a-dee-yo" instead.

In Texas, I found a pile of what looks like clay marbles in the middle of nowhere. Any idea what they are?

Little round balls of clay? Most likely armadillo poop. They eat insects and small snails, and in the course of picking them off the ground, they also eat a lot of soil. Their excrement is almost perfectly round. We're not sure if anybody has tried picking them up and firing them in kilns, but they could make a wonderful gift for children. Or not. This dirt-eating habit, by the way, is the reason that armadillo teeth are dark, sometimes even black.

Are armadillo bites painful?

To a bug or snail, armadillo bites are undoubtedly painful. However, to anything bigger, no. An armadillo's teeth are located at the back of its mouth, so biting is not part of its self-defense strategy. Good thing, too—it's the only animal besides the human that can carry leprosy.

Can armadillos swim?

Despite what has been commonly reported elsewhere, an armadillo can swim. The bony plates that protect an armadillo weigh it down, but it can still maintain buoyancy for short distances by gulping air to inflate its intestines. That said, it often prefers to cross small waterways by simply crawling along underwater.

Why are armadillos so commonly found as roadkill?

Unfortunately, most of the armadillo's defenses are completely unsuitable for dealing with cars. One of its strategies is to roll up into a protective ball completely surrounded by its armor, which can save it from a variety of natural things, but not an SUV. Another response is to dig straight into the ground, which it can do with remarkable speed in almost any soil type—but not, unfortunately, blacktop. Still another strategy is to leap straight

up into the air . . . which doesn't save the armadillo, but at least
gives it the small victory of making a wicked dent in a car's front
grill.

Sleepytime Bears

Do all bears sleep through most of the winter?

No, just those bears that eat more vegetation than meat, like
the brown and black bears. Their main food supplies die or get
buried under snow in winter, so it's a good time for them to go
undercover and live off their fat for three to seven months.
Polar bears, on the other hand, feed mostly on the flesh of seals,
so they can stay active and actually gain weight in the winter.

By the way, there is still some controversy over whether bears
actually hibernate, or if they merely go into a deep sleep.
Scientists on one side say that it's not true hibernation because
a bear's body temperature lowers only a little and because it can
be easily awakened. The other scientists point out that a bear's
heart rate drops to less than half its normal rate and insist the
high body temperature is a result of the bear's remarkably well-
insulated body. The debate rages on; stay tuned.

Are all black bears black?

Is this a trick question? Many black bears are, in fact, black.
However, black bears come in many colors, and even the black
ones often have a star-shaped white mark on their chests. For
the record, black bears can also be brown, bluish, cinnamon,
beige, blond, and even pure white. So why are they called black
bears? I suppose we can't blame the Dutch this time—it's
because more of them are black than any other color, and
before people realized that the other colors of bears were
actually the same species, the name had already stuck.

Are grizzly bears the biggest bear?

Second biggest. The mighty grizzly looks mighty puny when
compared to the Kodiak bear, its cousin from Alaska and
Canada. The average Kodiak bear weighs about 970 pounds;
the average grizzly only about 400. That's an average—the
biggest Kodiak ever measured was ten feet tall and 1,700
pounds. Not that you'd want to tease a grizzly about its relative
shortcomings—they're quite short-tempered and occasionally
live up to their Latin name, *Ursus arctos horribilis*.

How much time does a bear couple spend together during mating season?

Sometimes when you wake up one day and discover you've been living with a bear, it becomes clear that these things just won't work out, and it's time to separate. Bears live together for about a month and then go their separate ways.

What kind of bear did they use in the heyday of bearbaiting?

They used what we call *bruins,* which is (you guessed it) Dutch for "brown"—in other words, the European brown bear.

It's hard to understand the appeal of the bloody "sports" of the past. Bearbaiting was especially popular in London for several centuries, starting in 1174 and lasting through the supposedly sophisticated time of Elizabeth I and Shakespeare. The rules and outcome of the practice were chillingly simple: a bear was fastened to a stake, and dogs were let loose on it. Sometimes the bear was blinded, defanged, or declawed first; sometimes they left the dogs at home, and people whipped it and poked it with sharp sticks (while standing safely out of the range of its powerful paws). What makes the whole thing even more incomprehensible is that it was sanctioned by the king and Church, and in fact was considered an activity suitable for Sundays and holy days.

The sport died out in England during the late 1600s, and was finally outlawed in 1835.

It's disturbing to know that our ancestors took joy in such sadistic cruelty to a defenseless thing. It's even more disquieting to read reports that it's still going on illegally. The World Society for the Protection of Animals has collected stomach-turning accounts of present-day bearbaiting in Asian countries, with promoters adding such sick modern-day twists as the "dancing bear," in which a bear is forced onto a flame-heated metal plate. It suffers serious burns as it shifts desperately from foot to foot. This is accompanied by comical dance music, to the great amusement of the howling mob.

Pandering to the Bamboozled Masses

Are pandas carnivorous?

No, not usually, but they probably should be. Giant pandas, the
famous cuddly-looking black-and-white animals from China,
are related to carnivorous bears and in fact have a digestive
system—a simple stomach and short intestines—designed for
meat eating. How and why they came to be bamboo eaters is a
mystery that has not yet been solved.

One of the problems is that the panda's digestive system isn't
really well suited for bamboo, which passes through its body in
only five to eight hours, so the panda actually digests only about
17 percent of the vegetation it eats (a typical herbivore, in
comparison, digests about 80 percent). Furthermore, bamboo
doesn't have much nutrition to begin with. As a result, to
keep from starving, pandas have to eat an enormous quantity
of bamboo—as much as 85 pounds a day—necessitating a
near-constant cycle of sleeping and eating, both day and night.

Their bamboo fixation has cost pandas in other ways. They
will usually eat only certain varieties of the bamboo plant.
Species of bamboo die off in a cyclical pattern, and when the
pandas' choice of species becomes unavailable, they can starve
in large numbers. Still, individual pandas have been seen eating
other plants, chickens, and even, in one case, a leather jacket.
They have the reputation for entering villages and chewing and
licking cooking pots, which, 2,500 years ago, inspired the
folkloric belief that their diet consisted of copper and iron.
Despite their pickiness with bamboo, if allowed access to
human habitation, many will quickly adapt to human food,
from porridge all the way to pork.

How long is the panda's gestation period?

It varies widely from 97 to 163 days. The panda has a delayed
implantation cycle in which the fertilized egg can float free for
anywhere from one-and-a-half to four months before implanting
in the uterus.

Baby pandas are pink, naked, and very small, weighing a
mere three to four ounces at birth and looking, according to
one expert, "like ill-designed rubber toys." A panda mother
often gives birth to two cubs, but she usually abandons one to
die. She takes care of her baby so intensively, holding it safely in

her massive paws almost continuously for four to five months, that two would be too much. Although it sounds cruel, the second baby seems to be simple insurance in case the firstborn is not healthy enough to survive.

Are all pandas black and white?

Only the giant panda. The only other panda, called the lesser panda, is reddish. Although it lives in China and eats bamboo, scientists argue whether it's a panda at all. It is small, catlike, and more closely related—in both habit and DNA—to a raccoon than to the giant panda.

How Is a Gopher like a Waffle?

How did the gopher get its name?

Oddly enough, from the French word *gauffre,* meaning "honeycomb." Early French settlers called a number of burrowing animals by that name. (Hmm, this sounds familiar–see the question about groundhogs earlier.) It's not absolutely clear why, but attempts at explaining it have centered on the idea that gophers dig so many holes in the soil that it reminded the French settlers of a honeycomb. Or something like that.

The French seemed to like the name *gauffre*–they also used the same word for thin fried cakes with honeycomb patterns imprinted on them. In fact, linguists tell us that *gauffre,* after being dragged through the syrup of phonetic mistranslation by Germanic and English speakers, became the word *waffle.*

How do gophers see underground?

They don't, but luckily, they don't have to. They can run backward almost as fast as forward, and their hairless tail is very sensitive to touch, so they back through tunnels, feeling the way with their tails.

We Don't Need No Stinking Badgers

Where did the term to badger come from? Are badgers really that vicious?

If you're a gopher or a prairie dog, you might think so, because badgers like to eat them. However, that's not where the term comes from. It comes from a cruel sport called badger baiting, which is very similar to bearbaiting, described earlier. People once thought it was great fun to put a badger into a hole or barrel and set dogs upon it.

While the badger became nearly extinct in the late 1800s, it wasn't from badger baiting–it was because of the demand for shaving brushes. In those pre-canned-shaving-cream days, the bristles of badger fur were perfect for spreading lather.

What's a wolverine, exactly? Does Michigan have many of them?

A wolverine is an aggressive, badgerlike animal that lives in cold climates. It hunts animals as large as caribou by jumping on their backs while biting and slashing until they fall. Not a very admirable animal, so you have to wonder why Michigan would choose to call itself the Wolverine State. What makes the whole affair stranger still is that there are no wolverines living in Michigan; in fact, as far as anyone knows, no wolverines have *ever* lived in Michigan.

Historians tell us it's called the Wolverine State because of the fur trade. Michigan was a big fur-trading area by virtue of its location on the border of Canada and the Great Lakes. Canadians arrived bearing wolverine furs, which were then shipped to Europe. Since the return address read "Michigan," the outside world began associating the area with the animal.

But, hey, while you're at it, you might want to ask why the state next door (Wisconsin) is called the Badger State.

Okay, so why is Wisconsin called the Badger State?

Funny you should ask.

At least this state *has* badgers. Not a disproportionately high number, mind you, but you have to admit that Wisconsin has one up on Michigan. However, the state wasn't really called that because of its badgers (surprise, surprise), except indirectly.

"Badgers" became the nickname of lead miners who settled the state in the 1820s. Lead mining wasn't exactly a healthy or lucrative job that left a lot of time and energy for building houses. To deal with the harsh Wisconsin winters, a number of lead miners lived in caves that they'd dug into the ground and the sides of hills. The miners in their holes reminded people of burrowing animals, and thus they got the nickname "badgers," and so, eventually, did the state.

Life Imitates Disney?

Do meerkats really hang around with warthogs?
Been watching the *Lion King* video again, have you? No, meerkats hang around with other meerkats in meerkat colonies that resemble prairie dog colonies. Warthogs hang out with other warthogs, although older boars usually live completely alone.

Tapiring from Rump to Snout

What is the tapir's closest living relative?
Although it looks like a pig, the tapir is most closely related to the horse and the rhinoceros.

It's Gnus to Me

What's a gnu?
Not much. What's-a gnu with you? (It's another name for the wildebeest.)

How wild a beast is the wildebeest?
It's true that the name in South African means "wild beast," but you can't believe every tag the Europeans gave animals (see gophers, aardvarks, groundhogs, etc.). The wildebeest is a large antelope that roams through grassy plains of southern Africa, grazing in huge, usually placid herds. They come in two flavors—the blue wildebeest, which is quite common, and the black wildebeest, which has been hunted down to about 10,000 surviving members.

So why the "wilde beest" name? Well, they look scary, in the same way that American buffalo do. They

> Where can I see a picture of a wildebeest?

have massive bodies and bristly faces. When approached by a human, wildebeests will dash away to a safe distance, and then suddenly wheel around to stare menacingly back at the intruder. It's a scary thing to witness, but if you don't come any nearer, you probably won't have any trouble. We suppose you probably wouldn't want to be in their way if they were stampeding, but spread the gnus: the "wilde beest" has been given a bum rap.

Chocolate Moose with Squirrel

*My friend claims he saw a nature special that says
that the moose got its name from the French dessert.
Is he crazy?*

If not crazy, at least fatally misinformed. The moose got its name
from *moosu*, a Native American word from the Narragansett
language meaning "he who trims or cuts smoothly." The name
refers to the neat way moose strip bark from trees. Still, you have
to wonder about that. We're not here to second-guess the Native
Americans, mind you, but let's say you saw an animal that's bigger
than a horse and uglier than a cow, with a set of antlers that look
like the bony hands of God. Would your first, second, or even
tenth reaction be: "Wow, look at how smoothly he takes the bark
off that tree!"? We think not. So whether your friend is crazy or
not, we're curious about whoever was in charge of coining words
for the Narragansetts. Maybe they hired a Dutch consultant.

What is the largest species of deer?

Of the thirty-nine species of deer, the moose is the biggest.

*What are the chances that a moose will survive an attack
by a pack of wolves?*

Of the moose that a wolf pack stalks, only about one in twelve gets
killed. A moose is so good at defending itself that if it stands its
ground, wolves will back down. They're fairly fearless, those
moose: reports from Newfoundland years ago say they began
attacking train engines, running toward the iron beasts and
banging into them with their antlers. It took some time before the
train company realized that the attacks were seasonal, that the
attackers were male, and that not only did blowing the train
whistle not scare them, it seemed to make them madder.
Researchers finally figured out that the train whistle was the same
pitch as the moose mating call, and that the male animals were
seeing the engines as rivals. The railroads changed the pitch of
the whistles, and the moose attacks stopped.

Cue the Theme from *Rocky*

How does a flying squirrel fly?

Well, first of all, we need to establish that they don't really fly—
they drift like a hang glider from a higher branch to a lower

branch. The flying squirrel accomplishes this by using a fold of skin on each side of its body that's connected to its front and back legs. Leaping from a tree branch and stretching out its legs allows the folds of skin to become "wings" of sorts, but more like those of an airplane than a bird. A flying squirrel steers by using its flat, wide tail as a rudder and stabilizer. Its flight path begins with a sudden downward glide to pick up speed, then levels off, and finally makes a quick upward dart to slow down before landing. It's a skill that doesn't seem to require much practice: by the time they are six weeks old, young flying squirrels can fly on their own.

How far can a flying squirrel fly?

The higher they start, the farther flying squirrels can go before they hit the ground. The American flying squirrel has logged flights of 150 feet or more. However, the giant flying squirrel of Asia, measuring four feet instead of the nine to fourteen inches of its American cousin, can glide about ten times farther–1,500 feet, which is more than a quarter of a mile.

We Do What We Musk

What plant or animal does musk perfume come from— the muskmelon, the muskrat, the musk ox, or what?

Musk has been an ingredient in perfumes since ancient times, both for its own smell and as an oily base that, when mixed with more volatile scents, slows their evaporation. It's sort of strange that it has appeared in so many women's perfumes, since it's a male sexual scent, but that may just go to show that women buy scents they like, not necessarily ones the men in their lives find attractive.

Musk, for the record, comes from *muschka,* the Sanskrit word for testicle. However, the scent doesn't really come from an animal's testicles. Despite the many plants and animals that have musk in their name and natural odor, the musk used in perfumes comes from only one: the musk deer of Asia. The musk itself comes from a gland in the abdomen; to harvest it requires killing the musk deer and cutting open its belly. Luckily for the musk deer, scientists developed a synthetic musk in 1937 that has largely replaced natural musk in cosmetics. Unluckily, the deer is still being killed in large numbers because of an Asian superstition that its musk gland is an aphrodisiac.

Jen Fariello

ERIN BARRETT and **JACK MINGO** are the information wizards behind hundreds of articles and some twenty books, including *Just Curious, Jeeves; Just Curious About History, Jeeves; Dracula Was a Lawyer;* and *Doctors Killed George Washington.* They live in the San Francisco Bay Area, with kids, a cat, two guinea pigs, and a life-size cardboard replica of America's favorite virtual butler.

Isabel Samaras

MARCOS SORENSEN is the artist in residence at Ask Jeeves®, and is the creative spark behind the "Ask Jeeves" character. This work with Jeeves keeps good company with his other illustrations—ogle his portfolio at www.astrocat.com. In his free time he hangs out with his wife, Isabel, son Nico, and their great friends in the Bay Area.

SPENCE SNYDER is a versatile Mill Valley, California, illustrator. The great majority of his work has focused on fun and educational products for kids and young adults. Check out more of his work at www.spencesnyder.com.